MAY 23, 2008 09:24 a.m.
100-15 DITMARS BOULEVARD
EAST ELMHURST, NEW YORK

IN THE MATTER OF SIRHAN B. SIRHAN

SINCE IT MAY BE USED IN SENSITIVE LITIGATION
THIS DOCUMENT HAS BEEN
EMBARGOED IN THE SENSE THAT
IT MUST NOT NOW BE SHOWN TO ANY OTHER PEOPLE
OR ANY OTHER AGENCY PRIOR TO
THE TIME WHEN IT IS
ACTUALLY ADMITTED INTO EVIDENCE.

DR. W. F. PEPPER
ATTORNEY FOR SIRHAN B, SIRHAN
575 MADISON AVENUE, SUITE 10006
NEW YORK, NEW YORK 19922
BY: DR. W. F. PEPPER, ESO.

LAURIE D. DUSEK
ATTORNEY FOR SIRHAN B. SIRHAN
63-52 SAUNDERS STREET
REGO PARK, New York 11374
BY: LAURIE D. DUSEK, ESQ.

OCTOBER 14, 2009
IN ACCORDANCE WITH THE EMBARGO
SEVERAL PAGES AND REFERENCES
HAVE BEEN REMOVED
FROM THE ORIGINAL DOCUMENT
WHAT FOLLOWS REFLECTS THOSE CHANGES.

PROJECT ARTICHOKE

THE ZODIAC KILLER HOAX REVEALED

A TRUE STORY

By DAVID M. SILVEY

authorHOUSE®

AuthorHouse™
1663 Liberty Drive
Bloomington, IN 47403
www.authorhouse.com
Phone: 1-800-839-8640

First published by AuthorHouse 9/16/2010

ISBN: 978-1-4490-4468-8 (sc)
ISBN: 978-1-4490-4469-5 (hc)
ISBN: 978-1-4490-4470-1 (e)

Printed in the United States of America

This book is printed on acid-free paper.

This book is dedicated in loving memory to Dave Silvey. And to all other victims subjected to mind control. Your story is now told Dad, you can rest in peace now. We love you and miss you more each day.

CONTENTS

INTRODUCTION

This manuscript is an attempt to chronicle the observations and direct participation of one man to the events that led up to a psycho circus of U. S. government sponsored drug abuse, ritual child abuse, political assassinations and cult worship in America. Included is supporting information and documentation provided by Silvey, the media, public agencies, and other sources. The following manuscript is written by him and provides a first hand account of the interrelationship of activities and characters involved in MK-ULTRA – [Manufacturing Killers Utilizing Lethal Tradecraft Requiring Assassinations], the assassination of Robert F. Kennedy and infamous Zodiac murders in California.

Born in 1951, David Silvey grew up in Sunol California, during a time when there were an unusual number of unsolved murders and 'accidents' in the community. It was in Sunol that he met Bob Hemphill and Tom Pain [actual code names].

After the Korean War Dr. William J. Bryan, psychologist and reportedly chief of all medical survival training for the United States Air Force became a CIA consultant in the agency's experimentation with mind control and behavior modification, code name "ARTICHOKE." The Manchurian Candidate, a film directed in 1962 by John Frankheimer and starring Frank Sinatra, and later in 2004 directed by Jonathan Demme starring Denzel Washington, was based on MK-ULTRA and project Artichoke.

Silvey participated in a meeting at the Santa Rita farm safe house in Livermore with Zodiac murder victim Darlene Ferrin, who was also present at the Ambassador Hotel in Los Angeles at the time of Robert Kennedy's assassination in June 1968. "Ferrin also apparently knew her assailant according to several witnesses, including Michael Mageau, who was shot along side of Ferrin on July 4, 1969. Ferrin is the key to solving the Zodiac murders. But she is also the key to proving that the Zodiac was a hoax he was not a random killer, he killed for a purpose. Darlene had indicated that a big story would break in the newspapers around July 5, 1969. She had an argument with the suspect in a restaurant parking lot hours before she was killed and the suspect followed her and Mageau to the scene where they were both shot." [Napa Sentinel article by Harry V. Martin]

While in the service at Fort Lewis Washington, Aberdeen Proving Grounds Maryland, Hanau West Germany and Phu Bai Republic of Vietnam Silvey was repetitively visited or contacted by Bob Hemphill, who represented himself as a CIA operative; Silvey was threatened, coerced into drug and weapons exchanges and then re-mailing a Zodiac letter sent to him at Camp Eagle by Hemphill.

Overview

I last saw Zodiac murder victim Darlene Ferrin at her house painting party in Vallejo California on May 24, 1969. There were two overly dressed, strange men at Darlene's house that night, men that I have known about since the early sixties. She had met these two in 1966 at the Palace Hotel in Reno. One of the men was known to stalk family members and friends in the small town of Sunol where I grew up. Community members there including me, were afraid of him long before the infamous Zodiac killings. The other man - Dr. William J. Bryan was a psychologist and CIA consultant on the subject of mind control.

I personally know the Zodiac murders to be a terrible legacy of MK-ULTRA, the CIA's program of research in behavioral modification and mind control, and the umbrella for projects such as Artichoke and Operation Midnight Climax. These were two well-documented CIA projects that were administered from 1953 to 1969. CIA Teams used LSD and sometimes even poisons, to hypnotize subjects to kill someone while under its influence. Handlers recruited unwitting young people with drugs for adolescent prostitution. The prostitutes would slip LSD to un-consenting Bay Area residents and tourists in North Beach and then go back to a CIA safe house where the sexual encounter would be filmed. The Agency itself acknowledged that this testing made little scientific sense but it went on. The last thing those in charge wanted was accountability; the nature of these experiments placed the rights and interest of U.S. citizens in jeopardy, a serious violation of the CIA's charter.

The CIA mind control contractors who administered the behavioral modification experiments and the agents monitoring the safe houses for MK-ULTRA were in fact cold-blooded criminals, not qualified scientific observers. After the Korean War, the chief of all medical survival training for the United States Air Force, psychologist Dr. William J. Bryan reportedly became a CIA consultant in the development and the implementation of Artichoke.

A Federal Narcotics Bureau Captain and CIA consultant, George Hunter White, was assigned by Director Allen. Dulles in 1956 to supervise safe house operations. White, under code name 'Morgan Hall', established a safe house in the Bar Area; on Chestnut Street in San Francisco's North Beach, and lived on Green Street in Mill Valley with his wife. There was also at least one safe house in New York as well as the Santa Rita Farm near Livermore.

The CIA safe house that I am most familiar with is Santa Rita Farm, isolated in rural unincorporated North Livermore Valley and located in a covert area far removed from neighbors and completely surrounded by ranch land, hayfields, and vineyards. Upstairs windows were boarded-up and high voltage power supply was provided to the second floor where the team worked in a special operations room. Safe house staff included Ike Feldman who worked directly under George Hunter White and who is currently living in Long Island, New York. Feldman stated in an interview with author Richard Strattan for Spin Magazine in 1994: "The LSD... was just the tip of the iceberg. Write this down. Espionage. Assassination, Dirty Tricks, Drug experiments, Sexual encounters and the study of prostitutes for clandestine use. That's what I was doing when I worked for George White and the CIA.

Feldman first heard of George White while he was with Military Intelligence in Europe. White was with the OSS (Office of Strategic Services, forerunner for the CIA). I heard stories about him. Donovan (William Wild Bill Donovan, founder of the OSS) loved White. White had supposedly killed some Japanese spy with his bare hands while he was on assignment in Calcutta. He used to keep a picture of the bloody corpse on the wall in his office."

Black mail and murder were natural follow up when drugs or persistent cult coercive persuasion failed to ensure further participation. Hence, also on safe house staff behaviorally out-of-control U.S. Navy trained assassin code named Robert Hemphill, or 'Bob'. Bob who is an important character in my story consumed large quantities of drugs supplied by White.

On May 7, 1964, Pacific Airlines Flight #773 crashed in to the side of a hill near San Ramon. Because of the magnitude of the tragedy, and the fact that the smoke from the crash was so bad, the principal of Sunol Glen School, Pete Corona, canceled classes. From Sunol we could see the smoke from the crash just about ten or fifteen miles north of us. Life Magazine ran a big story about the incident with pictures in the May 22, 1964 issue.

The plane crashed within a couple of hundred yards of the big satellite tracking radar dish on the ridge top in San Ramon two towns north. It was one of the top ten worst California air disasters at the time and first significant use of hijacking as a 'terrorist' weapon in the United States. Unknown to me at the time, among the 44 victims were San Francisco Police Inspector George F. Lacau, San Francisco's Waterfront Bar and Restaurant owner Paul Marty and their wives.

Some years later, Bob Hemphill would reveal to me exactly how and why this plane crashed. According to Bob, 'Grand Chingon' William J. Bryan was legendary to 'insiders,' famous for his monstrous deeds in circles of ultimate evil. Bob often boasted [in bits and pieces] about helping Bryan, who was a former airline pilot, brainwash a Philippine national named Francisco Gonzales.

Hemphill stated that they recruited Gonzales in San Francisco with filmed adolescent sex, and then used blackmail to help program him with poison and hypnosis at Santa Rita farm. Bob told me that Gonzales was prepared by Bryan to crash a Reno-to-San Francisco bound commercial airliner into a satellite tracking station. Gonzales was drugged while at the Palace Hotel in Reno and triggered when the plane started to descend over the North Livermore Valley. According to the accident report, investigators discovered that Gonzales had advised both friends and relatives that he would die either Wednesday, May 6, or Thursday, May 7.

He referred to his impending death on a daily basis throughout the week preceding the incident. When the Fairchild F-27A (N2770R) with 43 other people started to descend over the safe house and mysterious ground-based wire antennae - Gonzales, fully triggered, pulled out his gun, entered the cockpit, and shot the pilot Ernest Clark. At 6:48 p.m. the aircraft radioed its last message, First Officer Raymond Andress was heard saying, "Skipper's shot. We've been shot. Trying to help."

Pacific Airlines Flight #773 actually flew over Santa Rita farm and crashed into the side of a hill near San Ramon. Bob suggested the whole terrifying tragedy was filmed below from the safe house. "We film everything."

White retired to Stinson Beach in 1965 and died in 1975. His diaries are maintained in a special collection at Stanford University's Green Library. The only diary missing in the large collection oddly enough is 1964. In a letter to CIA superior Dr. Sidney Gottlieb, White recounted safe house operations: "I was a very minor missionary, actually a heretic, but I toiled whole heartedly in the vineyards because it was fun, fun, fun; where else could a red blooded American boy lie, kill, cheat, steal, rape and pillage with the sanction and blessing of the all-highest."

Dr. Bryan lived in Sparks, Nevada, in the early 1960s and frequented the Palace Hotel where he met Darlene Ferrin and hired Bob Hemphill as a handler for Santa Rita Farm. By late May 1968, Zodiac victim Darlene Ferrin had knowledge of CIA Artichoke team involvement in conspiracy to induce an individual of Palestinian descent, under influence of Artichoke, to involuntarily perform an act of attempted assassination against a government official.

Just after midnight June 5, 1968 Senator Kennedy who had just won the California primary in his effort to secure the Democratic nomination, was shot in the pantry of the Ambassador Hotel on Wilshire Boulevard in Los Angeles. A female wearing a polka dot dress was standing next to the shooter. At 11:50 am the Los Angeles Police Department broadcast an APB emergency tele-type requesting information for the arrest of woman in the polka dot dress. The description was as follows: Female Caucasian, aged in the mid twenties, and around 5'6" in height, wearing a white violet dress, three quarter length sleeves with small black polka dots, dark shoes, bouffant-type hair.

Vallejo and Los Angeles Police Departments investigated accusations that a Vallejo woman was involved in the shooting of Kennedy possibly the girl in the polka dot dress. The accuser, according to the Vallejo Times Herald, was an anonymous woman neighbor. The officer said that he received a telephone call from a woman who suggested that my neighbor might have been mixed up in that shooting down south. But, the officer said, the woman who called would not give either her name or address, or the name of the woman she was accusing. (Excerpted from the Vallejo Times Herald June 6, 1968)

Moments later another woman called the same officer and said she was afraid she was being falsely accused. She was questioned and photographed. The photo was sent to LAPD.

Darlene Ferrin had knowledge of CIA Artichoke team involvement in the conspiracy to induce a subject, under influence of Artichoke, to perform an involuntary act of attempted assassination against Senator Robert F. Kennedy. The act was one of distraction, while a cold blooded assassin actually killed the Senator. The fact that Ferrin was a witness and participant became the motive to dispose of her at midnight July 4, 1969. Shortly after on July 31, 1969 the San Francisco Chronicle, the San Francisco Examiner and the Vallejo Times received letters from her killer.

Zodiac was introduced in a three-page letter in the part that was sent to the Vallejo Times Herald. August 1, 1969 the San Francisco Chronicle received a cryptogram from Zodiac. In the last line is code name 'Bob Hemphill,' but on the 4th line is his real name as it appears on the Zodiac suspect list. San Francisco Police Inspector Dave Toschi received a Zodiac cryptogram on November 8, 1969 that the NSA, CIA and FBI code breakers and computers couldn't solve. The first number is the number of rows, and the second number in the coordinate is the number of rows to the right, (4, 15) is 4 rows down and 15 rows to the right - 'RK.' 'K' is at the coordinate (4, 16). The date RFK was assassinated '6/5' is coordinate (6, 5) 'F' the missing middle initial for 'RK.' [Bookworm, see zodiackiller.

com - part of strand, internet entree 2003 approx] On the 10th row of the decoded version appears 'H LSD UL.'

In most CIA medical documentation H is the abbreviation for hypnosis, together with LSD UL it could possibly be referring to extremely sensitive and at the time Top-Secret MK-ULTRA behavioral modification technique. Combine un-decoded with decoded elements from cryptogram the message is clear – **RFK ASSASINATED UTILIZING LETHAL HYPNOSIS LSD - [ARTICHOKE].**

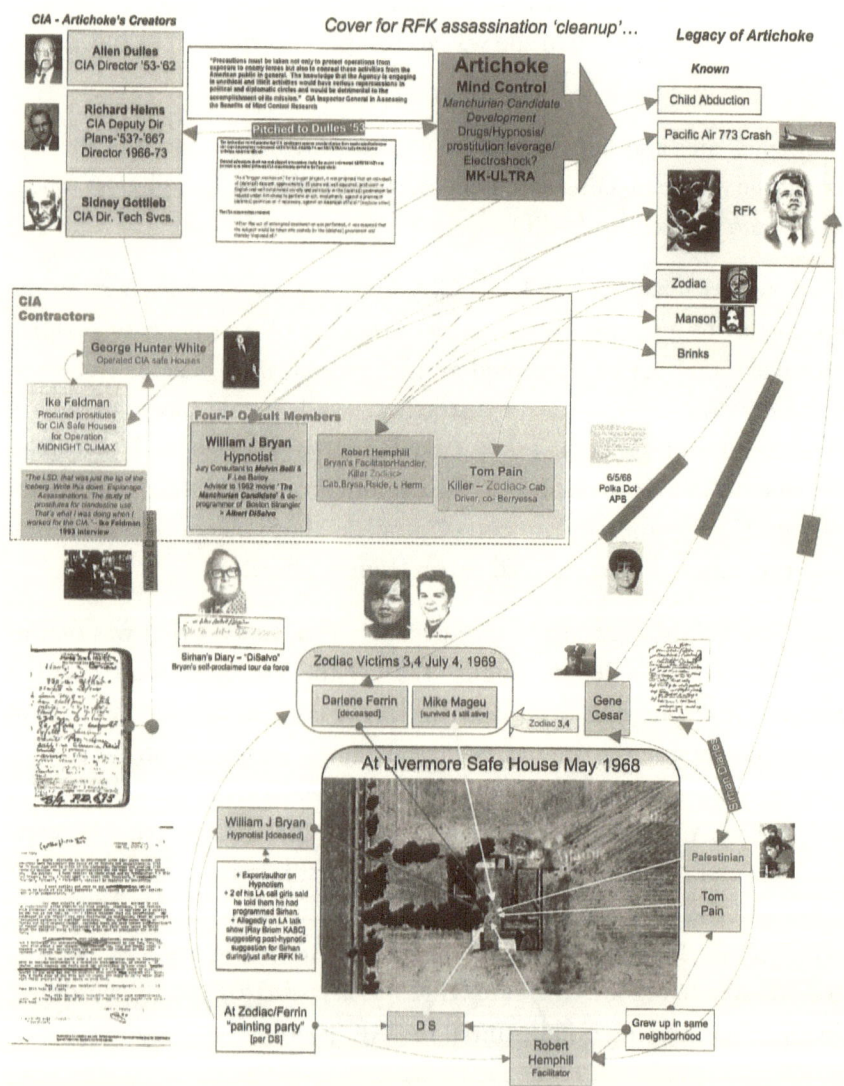

West Coast Safe House Supervisor
George Hunter White was aware of
this highly secret and remote
location. From his diary of 1959

The Early Years

I was born to Genevieve and Alvin Silvey on January 27, 1951 at Hayward Hospital in California. I was the third of four boys. My father was a blacksmith. He had a shop in the town of Alvarado and worked very long hours. From the beginning I was closer to my dad than my mother. I considered my father to be a kind person, a good dad, but rarely around. My mother was a traditional stay-at-home mother of the era she washed, cooked and generally looked after household affairs.

During my infancy decisions were being made in Washington D.C. by CIA Director Allen Dulles to conduct experiments on human beings; the nature of these experiments would place my rights and interest as a human being and U.S. citizens in jeopardy. The following CIA Office Memorandum has been released under the freedom of information act and is today archived by NSA at George Washington University in Washington DC.

22 March 1952: Memorandum for Assistant Deputy (Inspection and Security) Chief of Medical Staff. Subject: Experiments on interrogation techniques.

1. I have discussed with Mr. Dulles the proposed experiments to be conducted within the Agency on various interrogation techniques under the overall direction of OSI. I explained to Mr. Dulles that the Medical staff and I&S would backstop these experiments but that before doing so the approval of the Director or deputy Director has been requested.

2. Mr. Dulles agreed that these experiments should go ahead on a laboratory basis under medical and security controls which would insure that no damage was done to the individuals who volunteer for the experiments.

3. This memorandum will serve as your authority to proceed with OSI and TBS in the carrying out of these experiments. It is the understanding of this office that TBS will actually run the experiments and that OSI will provide supervision, device, and particular qualified personal.

6 May 1952: Memorandum for Chief, OSI and Chief, TBS. Subject: Sending of ARTICHOKE Team. Reference is made to discussions concerning the sending of an ARTICHOKE team to -----for application of appropriate techniques in regard to -------. The availability of the following facilities for ARTICHOKE, have been discussed with the interested case officers. However, it is suggested that the participants of ARTICHOKE be officially made known to the --------------- --------in order that appropriate advance arrangements and preparations might be made. The ARTICHOKE Team is prepared to depart around 22 May not more than two or three days from the 22 May date.

It is requested that the----------------- make the necessary advance arrangements to procure facilities as directed before in preparation for the arrival of this ARTICHOKE Team. The facilities desired are as follows:

House. A safe house should be obtained in which all actual operations can be carried out. The house should be large enough to accommodate a team of four persons, one or two case officers as determined by the chief of station and guards. Arrangements should be made for all personal to have meals on the premises so that operations can be carried on without the necessity of constant coming and going from the safe house for ordinary living purposes. Working area: Within the house the team will need two large size bedrooms with a full bath adjoining or nearby. The rooms should be on the second floor of the house. It is preferred that the rooms be well carpeted and with drapes if possible in order that there will be no outside noise, interference and the proceeding in the room can be properly monitored.

Location of the house: The house should be located in a safe and reasonably isolated area. However, it should be within reasonable distance of the station location for communication purposes and for the obtaining of any equipment and supplies deemed necessary in the course of the proceedings.

Guards: Security cleared guards should be provided on a twenty-four hour basis with ------------on the premises. The team is not in a position nor does it have the facilities to serve as guard for the subject, and accordingly, when the subject is not being processed, guard must be available for the security of the subject and house itself.

As a suggestion it is possible that the ---------arrangement of guards at a central area facility might be suitable for this operation without the security of going outside the official family unit bringing in mew personnel for this specific purpose.

Knowledge of the arrival of the teams and too location of the safe house and the proposed work of the team should be limited to only those personnel at headquarters and in the field who of necessity must have knowledge of this operation.

Under no circumstance should the mission of the team be circulated and become the subject of general discussion within the station. The team will bring with them all necessary equipment for the actual carrying out of the operation. The equipment referred to represents photographic, recording and other devices utilized by the team. The station will not be called upon to furnish any equipment in this line unless some unforeseen emergency develops.

Required time for the operation: After arrival of the team, two or three days should be allowed for the team to set up the safe house and confer with the case officers as to techniques to be utilized. The team can then agree upon the time the subject should be delivered to the safe house. It is estimated that a minim of four days will be necessary to conduct the processing of the subject, with a possibility of extending three or four more additional days.

Disposal: The techniques applied by the team will be in direct consideration of the disposal facilities available to the chief of station, and in those cases------------------ where definite disposal facilities exist, the team can utilize any form of technique. In other cases that might be presented where the disposal facility is weak and the subject may have full or limited degree of freedom following the processing, the team techniques will be adopted to the situation. In case, however, the team will discuss with the case officer and the chief of station, as necessary, the disposal factors prior to running of a case.

10. Techniques: It is in the full responsibility of the officer in charge of the team as has been stated are predicated on the security factors involved, disposal facilities available and the character of the subject.

11. Composition of the team: The team will be composed of a ------specialist who will be in charge of the team, a professional consultant to ------ a technician and a medical officer. A medical officer may be provided from headquarters or he may be assigned to the team from the field personnel by headquarters.

The following surviving 1954 CIA memo [that resembles in detail the circumstances surrounding the RFK assassination] reveals the cold-blooded criminal nature and intent of those involved in setting the focus and direction for the CIA's program of research in behavioral modification. The memo was declassified and released under the Freedom of Information Act then published in an article on Robert Kennedy's assassination by Lisa Pease in PROBE.

"The ARTICHOKE Team visited (redacted) during period 8 January to 15 January 1954. The purpose of the visit was to give an evaluation of a hypothetical problem, namely: Can an individual of ------- descent be made to perform an act of attempted assassination involuntarily under the influence of ARTICHOKE?

PROBLEM: a. the essential elements of the problem are as follows:

As a "trigger mechanism" for a bigger project, it was proposed that an individual of ------- descent approximately 35 years old, well educated, proficient in English and well established socially and politically in the ------- Government be induced under ARTICHOKE to perform an act, involuntarily, of attempted assassination against a prominent ------- politician or if necessary, against an American Official.

The SUBJECT would offer no further cooperation with (redacted). Access to the SUBJECT would be extremely limited, probably limited to a single social meeting. Because the SUBJECT is a heavy drinker, it was proposed that the individual could be surreptitiously drugged through the medium of an alcoholic cocktail at a social party,

ARTICHOKE applied and the SUBJECT induced to perform the act of attempted assassination at some later date. All the above was to be accomplished at one involuntary uncontrolled social meeting. After the act of attempted assassination was performed, it was assumed that the SUBJECT would be taken into custody by the ------- Government and there by "disposed of."

Another CIA document in 1954 referred to an experiment where a person could be transformed into an unsuspecting assassin who had a fear for firearms was brainwashed, and told to awaken another woman in deep hypnotic sleep.

"She was instructed that if the other woman would not get up, she should pick up a gun and fire at her. And she did exactly that and on cue went to deep sleep again. In the experiment, the gun was armed with blanks. When the ladies woke up, they could not recall the "shooting" event. On being handed the gun, the subject refused to handle it and denied that she ever participated in the event." [CIA MORI ID 19069 from Mathias Chang]

The Following CIA document describes operational use of sodium amatol and hypnosis for creation of amnesia barriers and deliberate insertion of false memories. It was released under the Freedom of Information Act to Dr. Colin Ross M.D. and presented in his lecture given at the 9th Annual Western Clinical Conference on Trauma and Dissociation, April 18, 1996.

"To Director of Security via Deputy Director of Security via Chief Security Research Staff from -------.

Subject: Report of Artichoke Operations 20-23 January 1955. Between Thursday 20 January and Sunday 23 January 1955, the Security Office Artichoke Team conducted special operations ---- ---. In the opinion of Team Members, in this case Officers of the -------, the Artichoke operation was successful. Details follow. It should be noted at this point that because these operations were the first Artichoke Operations undertaken in the USA, which is a violation of the CIA's Charter, the full names of those participating are omitted from this report and will not be revealed without consent of the Security Office.

First names, titles or pseudonyms will be used throughout this report. In view of the highly sensitive nature of the Artichoke techniques and in view of the fact that this was the first Artichoke operation carried out in the USA, the operation was conducted -------.

This Safe House is Far removed from surrounding neighbors, it is a large tract of land, and is thoroughly isolated. A limited, and security –cleared household staff maintain functions of the House and ------- by unwitting -------. Actual Artichoke operations as usual were carried out in a special area on the second floor of the House, and neither the household staff nor the ------- were permitted in the area during any of the processing. SSD Division furnished one security officer during the entire period of the operation to act as special guard and to handle any unusual situations,

Which arose during the operation. This guard is hereafter referred to as -------in this report. For a matter of record, it should be noted that the subject was not a confinement problem, and has been at all times fully cooperative. Guard detail was not present in connection with the subject, except in a general sense.

Technical matters in this case were handled entirely by the TBPSD under the personal supervision of -------. Full tape recordings were made of the entire case, and tapes are to be turned over to the participating Division in the immediate future. It should be noted that during this particular operation, a special device was used in conjunction with the recording.

This device, which is easily cancelable, worked with remarkable efficiency and at no time during the entire recording was there any break due to technical failure. It should also be noted that a complex two-way transmitting/receiving unit was again used in this Artichoke operation. Cover for the actual operation followed standard procedure.

The subject was informed in general terms that before being sent for further work it was necessary that certain tests be made on him physically and psychologically. Hence a complete physical and psychological /psychiatric examination was acquired. Subject readily accepted this medical cover and the Artichoke technique was introduced easily and with the full consent of the subject. The case: Prior to the commencement of the actual Artichoke operation, a number of conferences had been held with the various participating personnel involved. All hands had been briefed and procedures had been worked out. A general time schedule was prepared and operating instructions for Artichoke were issued.

On the afternoon of the 20ᵗʰ of January the subject and -------. They were met by -------- of the interested Division. Under a covert car subject was taken to the -------, arriving there at approximately 9:30 p.m. Prior to this, that is during the day of 20ᵗʰ of January, the technical equipment had been checked out and installed, and -------- had arrived at the covert area at approximately 8 p.m. for operational purposes. By previous arrangement the ------- was picked up by ------- at approximately 9:30 p.m. ------- ------- Was brought to the Safe House at 10:50p.m. shortly after the arrival of -------, a preliminary conference began approximately 11:10 p.m. with the subject.

Interrogation lasted until 12:25 a.m. when all except the subject ------- left the Operations Room Tape recording was cut off at this time. As a result of this interview -------stated that subject's mental and physical condition was good and noted that the pulse (Ross: which is actually the blood pressure) at 12:25 a.m. was 120/80 (Ross: so these guys are not total wizards). The doctor also commented he had noticed an increase amount of talk after a drink of whiskey and although there was some nervousness present, it was not excessive. ------- Stated he had given subject two grams of anibarbitol to the subject to assist him to sleep and it was later confirmed the subject had taken this prior to going to sleep.

(Ross: a half a paragraph is white out). Because of the successful penetration and because of the extremely high quality of information, which the subject was obtaining, the case is regarded as most sensitive and important by the participating Division. Since the subject's information had been checked and cross-checked many times by the Operating Division's Case Officers, and the Division was of the uniform opinion that the subject was fully legitimate and fully cooperating with our efforts; they however desired Artichoke to give added assurance to the subject's story and to help them determine absolute suitability for further use of the subject in his work. For the record, it should be noted that no polygraph techniques had been applied in this case, since a physical examination by ------- apparently a cleared physician had indicated too much nervousness for successful polygraph testing. Following established pattering using medical cover as explained above, the ------- began a physical and psychological examination at 10 a.m. on the morning of Friday 21 January.

This examination continued until 1 p.m. when an hour was taken for lunch. At 2 p.m. ------- again continued the general examination of the subject with ------- being used, as before lunch, as interpreter. This examination lasted until 3 p.m. When the ------- concluded the first medical session and a portable polygraph was taken in by ------- for the purpose of polygraph testing. (Ross: there's a bunch of blanked out stuff). On Saturday 22 January 1955 subject had breakfast with --------. At 9:35 a.m. ------- arrived at the Safe House and at 9:45 a.m. ------- arrived. At 10:35 a.m. the subject again, with ------- acting as interpreter, was examined briefly by Dr. -------. At 10:50 a.m. ------- left the operations area and began polygraph testing. This examination lasted until 12:37 p.m. when it was concluded.

(Ross: then it goes in --- I'll skip a little bit). Subject was taken into the Special Operations Room with only the ------- present and at 2:36 p.m. the first intravenous infusion began. Slow injections were continued until 2:46 p.m. when the ------- signaled that the subject was fully affected by the chemicals and at this time special recording and transmitting equipment was brought into the Operations Room. Also at this time ------- left the room and ------- entered. From this point until approximately 4:15 p.m. when the interrogation ended, Artichoke techniques were applied.

These techniques, which followed a previously agreed-upon plan, were in three stages: (Ross: this is now deliberate implantation of false memories).

Results during this phase were good and subject had no control. Time approximately 15-20 minutes. B. A fantasy in which -------. Results were again very good. Time approximately 40-45 minutes. C. Following development of the fantasies as noted above, the subject was more or less directly interrogated by -------, and ------- introduced as -------. Results only fair, although subject had little control. Time approximately 15 minutes. Immediately following the conclusion of the Artichoke treatments, a general conference was held with all hands present. It was agreed at this time that further Artichoke treatments were unnecessary, that results were as conclusive:

That in the view of the subject's importance, additional work with chemicals or with H technique might possibly antagonize the subject hence would be unwarranted and unwise. Following the conclusion of the general discussion all apparatus was removed from the premises, and all participating personnel with the exception of ------- left the area after the ------- had checked the subject. On Sunday 23 January between approximately twelve noon and 1:30 p.m., the --------, pointed out that the headache was a natural consequence of the "examination: and it would gradually disappear. In addition the ------- wrote a prescription which was to be picked up in another name for future use by the subject, as a general sedative. At 1:50 p.m. approximately ------- left the Safe House and the subject was turned over for handling to Case Officers of the participating Division.

CONCLUSIONS: In the opinion of the Artichoke Team the operation was profitable and successful. In this case the subject was aware that he had been given certain types of solutions but as to what he had been given or amounts given, he had no knowledge.

Checks were made by ------- and later ------- and apparently indicated that the subject, although not having specific amnesia for the Artichoke treatment, nevertheless was completely confused and his memory was vague and faulty. This vagueness and failure of memory was intensified."

DR. COLIN ROSS M.D.: "So that's obviously operational use of sophisticated mind control amnesia inducing and false memory implanting techniques in the USA in the 1950's by the CIA. It's part of a broad program of mind control research, experimentation and operational use, which included the creation of Manchurian Candidates."

Artichoke and Operation Midnight Climax were two well-documented CIA projects that were administered from 1953 to 1969. CIA Teams used LSD and sometimes even poisons, to hypnotize subjects to kill someone while under its influence. Handlers recruited unwitting young people with drugs for adolescent prostitution. The prostitutes would slip LSD to un-consenting Bay Area residents and tourists in North Beach and then go back to a CIA safe house where the sexual encounter would be filmed. The Agency itself acknowledged that this testing made little scientific sense but it went on.

Questions within my family:

I was baptized at the Old Roman Catholic Church in Alvarado. I'm not sure what the differences among churches were, but there was a church in town of that type so we went there. The priest wore brown robes with sandals. I remember midnight mass seemed magical spoken in Latin with incense burning. I was an altar boy, most people wouldn't remark about where or which church they baptized in, but as you'll see, in my life it mattered.

We lived behind my Dad's shop in a trailer near the railroad crossing on Hesperian Boulevard in Alvarado. We were about a mile north of town in an area surrounded by duck clubs, creeks and marshlands. The early years were good and it was great being a kid.

I had relatives living in the area. When we went to family gatherings or functions of my father's relatives, my father often only brought me along. If you were to look at the four boys you'd see a marked difference among our looks. I am the only one with the light complexion, blond hair and brown eyes of my father's side of the family. As a little boy this meant nothing to me. As a young man and then an adult I pieced together the reasons for this.

My oldest brother Alvin James Silvey Jr., nicknamed 'Ike' by my mother was like a best friend to me. He taught me how to hunt, fish, fight and play sports. As far back as I can remember my father and Ike never bonded and rarely spoke. The alienation that would last a lifetime even extended to my brother's wife Louis and the children. My mother had a friend named Ike; and she apparently nicknamed my brother after him. Sometimes we would picnic at the old secluded cemetery off Mission Blvd. in Irvington. We would have fried chicken, potato salad, and wine. My brother and I were allowed to drink Mogen David wine. My younger brother and I would benefit greatly from this get- together because after we drove Ike home near the cannery on A Street in Hayward. My mother would always take us to the toy store in Tennyson on the way home.

It was difficult to remember that my younger brother and I weren't supposed to mention outings with Ike. Retribution from my mother came in the way of ass whippings and threats of selling us instead of toy store runs at Tennyson. My younger bother Richard locked himself in the bathroom to avoid an ass whipping and she got the door open. He ran past her and away from home hiding in the marsh for hours into the night.

My parents were separated for a time and my mother started doing crazy stuff around the house like hanging dead chickens on the outside of our doors dripping blood at night.

She would also hang blankets over any mirrors during a full moon. It wasn't great for us being kids in Alvarado anymore. Both my older brothers moved out of the house and got arrested for robbing the post office in Alvarado.

Ike Feldman had a chicken ranch near the border of Alvarado and Fremont just off Highway 17 on Fremont Blvd... One day we stopped there to buy eggs, we drove into the dirt drowsy past barns and stopped. My mother told me and my brother to stay in the car. As my mother walked to the house a young kid my age ran to the car from one of the barns... He said his name was Jimmy and that his father brought him here and left. He started to cry and said they kill people here! Jimmy wanted to come with us and I let him in the car. Minutes later my mother came back to the car and saw Jimmy. I tried to tell her what he said but she dragged him out of the car and we left Jimmy crying. She pulled over just past the fruit stand and she whipped my ass. I didn't want to cry out of defiance but her knuckles were boney and caused incredible pain on my face, head and back.

Abducted at eight:

It was a nice day: I had just celebrated my eighth birthday and was in third grade at Alvarado Elementary. I had just got out of school. In northern California's Bay Area it doesn't snow, it mostly just rains a couple days a week and is often cloudy and cool the remaining days in winter. Since the weather is mild kids can walk to and from school if they live nearby. I was walking home and was alone.

As I was walking by the Old Roman Catholic Church a young priest whom I had never seen before stepped out onto the sidewalk between the church and a car parked in front on Main Street. The priest said to me, "you're going to help us on the farm today. Your mother is already out there, you can ride in the back seat." He opened the back door but it didn't feel right and I was kind of scared. I looked at his brown rode, his sandals, and at the church where I was baptized, where I went to Mass. I got in the back seat, and as he shut the door I noticed an army blanket folded neatly on the floor with pieces of cut rope. The priest got into the front of the car and looked back and said, "You get down on the floor." He appeared different with a menacing look on the face, I couldn't move. He back-handed me hard in the face and said it to me one more time. I got down on the floor, my nose was bleeding and I was crying uncontrollably.

As we drove past the school I stuck my head up to see if anyone was watching. The priest stopped the car on the railroad tracks and reached around to tie my hands behind my back then threw me on my back on the seat and hit me hard in the groin. We drove for what seemed like an hour then he stopped the car. I looked up to see as he got out of the car, then he came around and opened the passenger side back door at my feet. I noticed that the door and window handles were missing the priest told me to get out. As I did a mangy looking black German shepherd bit my leg.

I began to run in a tight circle with my hands still tied behind my back around the car. I turned to see an ever-haunting horrific sight. I saw a little girl my age with a monstrous look on her face, her head was shaved and bruised; she had two wires coming out of the top of her head. She was on the attack growling and showing her teeth just like the dog.

A big guy with dirty blonde hair wearing those black-rimmed glasses that men of the era wore put the girl inside the barn near the house and then ran the dog off. We were all still near the car as the priest told another man (whom I recognized as my mother's friend Ike) dressed in khaki clothing wearing aviator-type sunglasses) told the big guy that he wants $3,700. The big guy came over to me and asked if I had been baptized. I said that I was baptized. The priest was paid $2,700 for me. Ike counted the money on the hood of the car. The priest told them that he was on his way to Arizona and left. At this point Ike told me, your mother sold you and she doesn't want to see you anymore. You belong to this man now do you understand!

All I knew about these people convinced me that they might do to me something like what had been done to the little girl. I completely bought what Ike said; my mother had often threatened to do just that. Over and over, to myself, I said prayers that I had learned in church, while the man untied my hands. Then we went in through the back door of the house and sat at the kitchen table. There was an old couple in the kitchen cooking. They said nothing to me nor did I to them. They talked at each other using no names.

The big man went to the refrigerator and returned with some red kool-aid, several sheets of paper and some pens. He asked if I could write something for him. I was shaking so badly that I had great difficulty writing the last two words and doing the art work. Investigator and Author Maury Terry found the letter many years later at a satanic site in Fire Island, New York and published it in his book Ultimate Evil. I wrote the following per his yelling instructions.

Woe is you O
Earth and sea, for
The devil sends the
Beast with rath,
Let him who has understand

Recon the number of the
Beast, for it is a human
Number its umber is
Six hundred and
Sixty Six,

He poured about half a glass of kool-aid and gave it to me. I drank it quickly and soon feel asleep at the kitchen table. I woke up the next morning near what looked like a dentist chair. I was on a sofa in front of the up-stair's window. I could see the rangeland gently sloping up to mountains a couple miles away. I would soon find out first-hand that there was a gun range just to the east of the neighboring eucalyptus grove. When I got up to go to the bathroom I didn't see anyone until I opened the bathroom door and saw the big man. He handed me a little bit of kool-aid and said let's go get something to eat! I followed him out the back door to a black Cadillac parked at the south side of the farmhouse. I opened the passenger door and got in. I noticed the door and window handles were there. We drove out the eucalyptus tree-lined driveway and made a left turn onto the roadway. As we came to a cross street I strained to see the road name, it was Mary School Road. He didn't say anything to me about it, but he noticed.

A couple of miles down the road he turned left into a driveway to the closest neighbor's farmhouse. An old man was signaling us to drive near the barns behind the farmhouse and that's where we parked. The old man opened the barn door and we got out of the car then went inside. The big man ordered me to pull my pants down as he pulled his down. His penis was huge and white like wax, I felt the old man looking at me like I was a woman. My thoughts went to extremes: from prayer to how to save my soul if not my life, to fantasies of vengeance to ' just getting through the physical and emotional trauma... The old man had open sores on his penis. I started to feel the effects of my first acid trip. It felt like I was crawling out of my skin.

I remember we got into the car and drove back to the big farmhouse where he drove into the yard then parked next to the barn. He got out and opened the barn door; I got out of the car and began to run away when he grabbed me by the neck then carried me inside the barn. He dropped me in front of a large wooden box.

He took the lock off the clasp and opened the door. He then grabbed the little girl and pulled her out of the box. He told me to get up and get in the box. I got up and saw the hellish sight, inside was part of a child's torso with guts and a big live snake. I couldn't bring myself to get in and he stepped forward to pound on me so I got into the box. The beast closed the door and I heard him attach the lock to the clasp. I had to take short breaths, it smelled terrible and there wasn't enough room to sit up (4' by 4' and 3' high) so I had to lie down. I had dry heaves real bad, I couldn't even cry. It seemed like hours went by before the snake got active and bit me on the face then the thigh. The snake stuck to my pants so I was able to grab it. I was choking it as hard as I could when I heard the lock being removed from the clasp. I pushed the door up with my head to see the little girl. She had wires sticking out of her head with a normal warm human look on her face. She was using her hands motioning for me to get out.

I looked at the incredible colors of the snake as I tossed it aside and quickly got out of the box. The front barn door was locked from the outside so I ran around looking for a place to break out. I started kicking one of the boards on the south barn wall. I got down and charged it with my shoulder and was able to push the bottom of the board out enough to escape. I saw the little girl's hands pull the board back in place from inside. I ran south as fast as I could. I soon heard gunshots and closed my eyes but kept running.

I crashed into a barbed wire fence but was able to get myself free, continuing to run southeast through what I would later find out to be a Lawrence Livermore Radiation Laboratory experimental ground-based wire antennae field. It was a massive area of poles and wires. There was a fence with green posts and white tips and signs warning that I was on FCC property. I ran into fairly new homes and pounded on a couple of doors before a man answered his door and I pretty much dove onto his living room floor.

I tried to tell him what happened but I could hardly breathe. The man told his wife to call the police and tell them that I had been kidnapped. She came into the living room and told him that the Livermore Police won't come out because we were in an unincorporated area. He told her to try the Sheriff's Department. A Sheriff's deputy showed up and took me to Hayward Hospital.

Dr. David Crocket examined me, the same doctor who delivered me eight years ago. I told him and the Sheriff's deputy everything that had happened. I was relieved to be free but deeply depressed about the little girl.

From this point on and through the rest of my childhood I would not be able to sleep without a light for fear of waking up in that box. They took my clothes all stained with visceral fluids then treated me for the bites, barbed wire cuts and sexual trauma. This all took days and no one came to see me, then a man dressed in a dark suit came into my hospital room to tell me that he would be taking me home. "Relax you'll see your mother shortly." Dr. Crocket introduced the heavy-set policemen to me as Captain White... I asked him why there was no door handle as we left Hayward Hospital in the black sedan. He said nothing just got on Highway 50 toward Stockton then exited on North Vasco Road in Livermore. He made a left turn into the area of houses that I ran to, then he wanted to back track. We drove past the gun range then up May School Road to North Livermore Avenue.

When he drove past the farm where I had been taken to, I pointed to the barns and he pulled over in front. "This is where you were? A doctor lives here! You're making this all up." He shoved me hard against the door.' How do you know Ike?" I told him that he was a friend of my mother. "Your mother is a whore?" He made a U-turn and drove while glaring at me most of the way to Alvarado.

He let me out of the car and on the way to the trailer threatened to kill me if I keep lying. My mother acted broken and surprised. "They didn't call me to come pick him up!" White told her that I was fine and made all this up." He is a runaway". White further stated that I made serious allegations concerning a doctor to the Sheriff's Department and that I was lying, "He should be taken care of. I never want to hear anything more about this again." Captain White asked to use the restroom, when he returned he took me outside and told me he had left two guns in the closet under towels, "You hide them, when the time comes you'll know what to do with them." I did what he said.

This was so emotionally draining and ever haunting that we never spoke of it again until forty-five years later. After my father's death when my mother apologized for her being evil and hurting me as a child, consumed with tears she admitted to selling me.

My Parents [below]

GROWING UP AROUND
CULTS THAT KILL

In 1963 we moved to Sunol from Alvarado, also in the East Bay of Alameda County. Sunol is a tiny little town set among the hills and valleys about 30 miles southeast of San Francisco and five or so miles south of Pleasanton.

During the 1960s the town of Sunol reported an unusually high number of unsolved murders and accidental deaths - mostly by fire. More than seven people that I knew were killed in 'accidents' in Sunol between 1963 and 1969: Joe Monighetti was burned to death in his trailer. Jimmy, Joe Monighetti's friend also burned to death in a tractor accident near what is now the Sunol Valley Golf Course. Cliff Fisher was run off the road in Niles Canyon. Lee Coen burned to death in an accident where Joe died.

In and around Sunol there were other strange, violent, and cultish occurrences and characters that I personally aware of, as well as many that my brothers and friends have told of over subsequent years.

My first encounter with Tom Pain:

In 1963 I first met Tom Pain, one of the neighborhood kids. Tom lived with his parents and brothers on Old Foothill Road in Sunol. Tom was five years older than me. He was about seventeen at the time, 5'11 athletically built, and weighed probably two hundred pounds. He was the second among six brothers and clearly not like the others in temperament. Tom was odd in that he was preoccupied with death and often spoke of killing. Bob Ussery, a local friend, and I were hunting squirrels one day in 1963 at the end of Bond Street in Sunol when we encountered an armed Tom Pain. Tom began talking about his knowledge of killing people and played out various techniques in front of us.

Tom stated, "In another life and time I was the greatest killer of all." As we all walked back toward town, Tom approached a car parked on the dirt road. Without warning, he ran up to the car and through the open passenger's window and fired on the driver's side repeatedly with his .22 caliber rifle. Tom then reached through the window with his knife and in frenzy stabbed the passenger seat ten to fifteen times. It looked and sounded very strange as he growled deeply throughout the entire incident. After this was over, Tom acted differently somewhat despondent. We (Bob and I) watched him carefully; concerned that he might possibly turn on us. When we returned to town Bob Ussery stated to me that Bob Hemphill (another Sunol guy) does the same kind of things; all the time talking about killing people but with him its kids. "I saw Hemphill kill a horse just like that - all of a sudden."

January 27, 1964: on my birthday we buried my brother Leroy; an apparent suicide.

Crash of Pacific Airlines Flight #773:

On May 7, 1964, Pacific Airlines Flight #773 crashed into the side of a hill near San Ramon. Because of the magnitude of the tragedy, and the fact that the smoke from the crash was so bad, the principal of Sunol Glen School, Pete Corona, canceled classes. From Sunol we could see the smoke from the crash just about ten or fifteen miles north of us. Life Magazine ran a big story about the incident with pictures in the May 22, 1964 issue.

The plane crashed within a couple of hundred yards of the big satellite tracking radar dish on the ridge top in San Ramon two towns north. It was one of the top ten worst California air disasters at the time and first significant use of hijacking as a 'terrorist' weapon in the United States. Unknown to me at the time, among the 44 victims were San Francisco Police Inspector George F. Lacau, San Francisco's Waterfront Bar and Restaurant owner Paul Marty and their wives.

Some years later, Bob Hemphill would reveal to me exactly how and why this plane crashed.

Killings associated with Tom:

During the summer of 1965 Tom was in the Navy stationed in Southern California. At times when he was at home on leave, he spoke of being a hit man for the Mafia. He often bragged about having connections down in Los Angeles. Tom was once home on leave because he was facing arson charges in Alameda County Superior Court. He bragged to me that he killed an individual named Joe Monighetti. Tom stated, "the old fuck was living down Niles Canyon. We fired his trailer up with rifles then torched it with gas. We could hear screaming - it was fun."

I asked him why he did it. Tom responded, "For Gilbert, Joe fucked him over and we got even." Joe was killed on June 26, 1965 and I after found out that what he said was true except Tom wasn't there. Lee Coen and his son, Conrad Trevino lived near Joe's trailer and then spoke of this incident as stated by Tom but Lee Coen described it differently, "That bastard (referring to Tom) wasn't there. It was Gilbert Andrade with others that murdered Joe. We saw the whole thing but you can't say anything or they will come after you." Lee told me this while he was pumping out the septic tank at my parent's ranch in Sunol. Conrad and I talked about it afterward and he said that they (Conrad and his mother Juanita) tried to stop the attack.

On May 28, 1966, Lee Coen was killed in an accident by fire near the same place Joe died. Also in the spring of 1966 Tom got out of the Navy and bought an almost new 1966 ice blue Chevrolet Chevelle from Tony Pine. He had gained weight, grew a beard, and no longer wore the horned rim glasses that he had always worn. I ran into Tom a day later when he was driving a 1952 tan/gray Studebaker Commander full dress with a window-mounted water cooler and gray exterior sun visor. Tom opened the trunk and I could see antiques such as candleholders and jewelry inside. Tom spoke about being accused of arson for small fires in Sunol.

He stated, "I got to kill some motherfucker over that." Trying to change the subject, as I had ratted on him to the Sheriff's Department months before, I asked if he was home for good. He stated, "I am going to college down in Southern California and might have job down there with Bob's (Hemphill's) relatives in the maintenance department at Riverside City College. Gene, Bob's friend, is looking into some work at Lockheed for me too."

I meet Bob Hemphill:

One day in September 1966, Tom asked if I could get some weed, bennies and reds for his friend, Bob. We'll be waiting at (Hemphill's) when you can get it. A friend of mine had what he wanted so we went to deliver up to Kilkare Canyon. Just past the first small bridge we saw Tom and Bob in the driveway. Hemphill appeared to be about thirty five years old with fine dark hair in a pompadour and piercing dark eyes. He was wearing black-rimmed safety glasses with a rubber band across the back. He was about 5'9' tall and approximately 165 lbs. Noticing Bob's bell-bottom pants and his shoes my friend asked if he was in the Navy. Bob pointed to a framed picture of a Navy ship mounted on the wall of the garage workshop.

Bob stated, "I was an electrician on the Liberty." He seemed so proud I asked why he didn't stay in the Navy. "I was falsely accused and convicted of murder and then trained by the Navy as an assassin in San Diego and released." He bought a quarter pound of weed and several jars of cross-tops without smoking, smelling or even looking at it Tom took off in the Studebaker as Bob said to me, "I wanted to meet Gilbert! Tom won't introduce me to him. He says Gilbert doesn't want to meet me. Have you heard that?" I told Bob that I really don't know Gilbert. Bob stated, "It's important that I talk to him. He knows that he and I are into the same thing." I questioned him on that and he said, "I like killing, I like to hunt them. I like it personal and bloody. They are a bunch of chicken shits, they like crowds and things like fake accidents and fire I don't want to join them. I just don't want them thinking that I'm trying to get into their territory." I thought this guy must be full of shit.

However, I knew where Gilbert lived and offered to take Bob to his house. Bob, my friend, and I got into a late model bronze Olds with red interior (owned by Bob's aunt visiting from Southern California) then drove down Bond Street and parked in front of Gilbert's house. He was standing in the front yard staring at us while watering his plants. He flipped us off and Bob started to get out of the car. Gilbert dropped the hose and walked into the house. Concerned that he went inside to get a gun I insisted that we leave fast. Bob took off at high speed and said, "If you guys weren't here I would have dropped him." Bob pulled a handgun out from under the seat. It was a blue steel semi-auto Browning 9mm (old).

I looked at the handgun peculiar as it was; there were grooves machined into the receiver. The barrel stuck out past the slide and was threaded. I questioned him about the grooves. Bob pulled over in front of his house at 21 Kilkare Road, got out and opened the trunk. We got out and he showed us a wooden stock attachment and slid it onto the receiver. Bob went on, "That's how they made them during the World War. It stabilizes your aim for night shooting I attached a scope mount and special pen light it's deadly with the silencer." He also showed us a cheap Harrington & Richardson .22 Caliber Revolver and a High Standard .22 Caliber model 101 semi-auto. Both guns were badly rusted and I recognized them as the ones that I sold to Tom just after moving to Sunol in 1963.

Tom Pain together with Bob Hemphill:

October 1966 Bob was in town, just back from New York. He asked if I could help him get some more dope. He asked for a quantity of weed, reds cross-tops and LSD. I want my girlfriend to try some acid. I got in touch with my friend and we went to Hemphill's place at the rear of 211 Kilkare Road. After the incident with Gilbert my friend was very apprehensive about having anything more to do with him.

Bob bought one kilo of weed, two jars of cross-tops and five tabs of white Owsley LSD. He bought it all and paid an incredible price. It was like he had an endless supply of money for drugs.

Greed gave way to concern in our minds when we observed Bob's hands were shaking and he had a feverish look about him. My friend, Dave Mullins asked Bob is he used the drugs himself. Bob said I smoke a little weed by myself at night and when I watch TV. Women like the cross-tops so I keep them around.

My friend asked Bob if he ever dropped acid before. "Why, what's the deal, what the fuck's up with you?" We suggested that he not take more than a quarter-tab and have somebody around that he can talk with. He got even more upset, "Don't fucken worry about it asshole." My friend said, "Maybe I'll keep the acid." Bob's eyes and face were filled with full-blown fury. I guess he thought we were making fun of him. Bob was wearing a T-shirt and looked unarmed. After seeing his reaction we both knew letting him keep the acid was a bust.

We believed he may do something really crazy, even for him while under its influence and get us busted. During our conversation an oxidized light green Studebaker pulled into the driveway. It was Tom, our hope of getting back the LSD diminished - he was always armed. Tom opened the trunk of the green Studebaker and the two of them (Bob and Tom) looked into it. I walked over to check out the car and Bob slammed the trunk shut. I asked Tom what year it was and he said it was a 1947.

I meet Bob's friend Thane E. Cesar:

The paint was oxidized but it was in great condition and the seats were perfect. It had an American Airlines parking permit on the passenger side window. I asked Tom is he was working at the airport and he responded, it's not my car, it belongs to Gene Cesar it's his baby later that evening I saw the same car in town Tom, Bob, and Thane Eugene Cesar at the wheel.

They got out, Cesar a WMA (Cuban) heavy set with a big head, about 25 to 30 years old, 5'8', 180 lbs., dark hair and eyes, was wearing a heavy canvas type navy jacket. Bob introduced Gene to a few of us in front of the store; they called each other ' cuz'. I reached out to shake hands and he just walked past me into the store. Bob told me that he doesn't like meeting people. You guys should leave. Two years later Thane Eugene Cesar would be Robert F. Kennedy's security guard, standing right behind Kennedy, the night he was assassinated.

I saw Tom a few days before Halloween, October 1966; at Old Foothill Road as he was getting into his mothers white 60' Ford Falcon. I stopped to say hi and noticed how curly his hair was, it looked like a woman's hair it was premed and he had a full beard. I laughed it was so inconsistent with his hard guy image. I asked how college was going, and he replied, "Fucked just like you." He then drove off peeling gravel all over me.

More stories and suspicions:

I was sixteen years old in early 1967 when I saw Bob and Tom working feverishly to pull the motor out of Gene Cesar's light green Studebaker at 46 Kilkare Road. They left the motor on the ground near the old blacksmith shop behind the house (where it would remain for years). As with everything involving these two people, there was something fishy about the fact that they removed the motor from Cesar's car for several reasons: First, the hasty manner in which they seemed to be working; and second, I knew the owner of the house at 46 Kilkare, Oscar Postel. He was one of the two people who told me about Bob's shooting the horse to death and when he described it he made it clear how much he disliked Bob. He would never have let Bob use his place. I came to believe they were removing the motor that day and having the car towed away to Joe Hemovitch's land next to the Sunol Golf Course because they wanted to remove the serial number connection from the car. I saw the car later and saw that the passenger side seat was all cut up like the seat that Tom had worked over in 63'. Also, the windshield on the passenger side was broken from the inside out.

Gene Cesar's 47 Studebaker "Baby" [below],

As they towed Cesar's car away that day Bob again stated that he just got back from New York and that he wanted me to come up to his place. I told him that I was about to leave town. With a menacing grin on his face, he ordered me to bring weed and several jars of cross-tops. I picked 'the order' up and went to Hemphill's at 211 Kilkare Road. My friend who was with me, the one involved with the confrontation between Gilbert and Bob, wanted nothing more to do with Bob. While making the delivery, a friend or relative of Bob's confronted me in the driveway. He was WMA, in his twenties and about 5'10' in height, 175 lbs. with light brown hair. He was angry and wanted to fight...

"So you're the son of a bitch, I know your family well. Bob is sick in the head, what's wrong with you? You don't see that Bob is nuts and he is driving his mother nuts. He steals money from her to buy your damn dope. We suspect that he may have killed a girl. If you don't stay away from him, I'll call the police and have you arrested. If I have to turn Bob in, you and that long hair punk are going to jail."

That same evening Bob was in front of the store in town his face red with anger. He said to me and other present, "you guys want to go to a party tonight?" I said "no" and the others didn't say anything. I informed Bob that I didn't want any trouble with his family or the police. Bob fell apart "There is going to be a party with a lot of women there, I need the dope." He went on speaking but the words made no sense, like chewing me out it must have sounded okay to him. He stood there beaming at me like he expected me to answer. I felt bad. I felt that my supplying him with drugs was making him nuts especially after the encounter on Bob's driveway earlier in the evening. I really felt terrible I thought about what his friend or relative had said about Bob. I was ashamed and worried about what was going to come of this Bob may have been involved in killing a girl. Wow, and in some strange way I may have had something to do with it.

It was after this incident that I started keeping these notes so I could prepare a statement if I was ever arrested. A few days later, David Mullins and I were driving toward home, southbound on the Pleasanton Sunol Road a couple of miles north of the center of town. It was late at night as we approached the second narrow railroad bridge. I noticed a vehicle parked on the road under the bridge with lights off. As we got closer, the vehicle took off, head on towards us. I drove off the road and hit the railroad embankment hard. Several individuals were running east from Sunol up the railroad tracks toward us yelling, "Chicken shit motherfuckers, fucking dope addicts, you bitches are going to die." Some of them had rifles and one had a gas can.

Mullins and I got out of the car and ran north along the road towards Pleasanton. Within a couple of minutes, a highway patrol officer stopped. We pointed to the wreck of my International Scout, which was now on fire, and watched as they ran down the railroad back toward Sunol. The CHP officer called the Sheriff's Department. Later in Sunol we recognized some of the individuals in the incident and later met one of them, the one who had been carrying the gas can. Mullins grabbed him by the throat and asked who the others were. He stated, "Bob Hemphill hot-wired his neighbor's old 40' Nash and was the driver. Gilbert, Tom and some badass people from a gang called Al Hilal were on the railroad tracks. They got like a contract on you guys. The more tyrants they kill the higher in the group they go." This is a sect of west coast avengers who according to him believed Jesus employed hypnosis to perform many of his miracles; they called this "Magic." They worship satin and are hell bent on fulfilling prophecy and assassinating tyrants in the name of God

On July 9, 1967, Hemphill's across-the-street neighbor, Cliff Fisher, was killed in an accident in Niles Canyon near the place Joe and Lee Coen died. Someone ran Cliff off the road down an embankment his vehicle landing upside down on the railroad tracks...

My friend Dave Mullins moved to a basement apartment in the Mission District of San Francisco, thinking it would be harder for them to follow or make an attempt on his life. Soon after, he told me that he saw Hemphill following him on Haight Street.

San Francisco Haight-Ashbury District 1967, the Summer of Love.

I regularly visited friends in the Haight and I did see Bob Hemphill there. The first time I saw him in San Francisco he was wearing a strange kind of ball cap, it was black with a Mendez goat head in red on it and he wanted to talk. "I'm not into drugs anymore we got something deeper happening, you can be a Master." I asked what he was talking about and he stated, "Gilbert and those assholes he hangs around with are making Tom a member. They are killing anyone that knows about Tom's handy work."

In the San Francisco Bay area during the 60's the climate of gang stalking was virulent and it included the Hells Angels, Black Panthers, Oakland PD and gang-cults of CIA creation. To survive their social filters and mind control I remained a Sunolian; hyper vigilant martial arts proficient beer drinking student of Zig-Zag Zen.

The Occult, Black Market
And Charles Manson

Tom inducted into occult worship group:

That same summer a God-fearing devil-worshipping ritual ceremony brought Tom into Al Hilal. It was held at Gilbert Andrade's place near the end of Bond Street in Sunol. I was at Jerry Lee Gratin's trailer just up the street. She and I saw expensive cars followed by a pick-up with several flags furled on poles arriving at Gilbert's, Tom's brother stopped by and told us about it. "Many of them are armed; some were dressed in brown ceremonial robes like friars and other were dressed in masquerade costumes. Armed guards dressed in black, formed a roving triple perimeter."

Bob pulled up on his Harley to Jerry Lee's trailer and joined us. His link with Al Hilal up to this point was access to the black market. He boasted "I can get anything evil." Bob claimed to have Luciferian Degree of Master in a group called 'The Process': "I keep the FOUR P Grimoire, a journal of evil deeds that the group did." The Grimoire included personal information about the participants and victims; pictures of friends, family members, or enemies. Information was held for use in blackmail, and threats of public exposure and physical harm or death to individuals or loved ones.

Bob introduces me to Charlie Manson:

Sometime in the fall of '67 my friend David Mullins and I were in the Haight looking to score drugs when we saw Bob near the Straight Theater wearing his black cap with the red goat head symbol and a blue work shirt with the 'Bob' nametag. He said that he could get us into the Equinox of the Gods a show that was playing with a band called Oz. He was with part of the group producing it. We told him that we had just come into the city to score then we were driving back to Sunol.

Bob said that a friend of his was staying down the street and had whatever we wanted. We walked to the corner of Haight and Stanyan where there was a black brush-painted bus with a red goat head painted on the front windshield, just like the one on Bob's hat. I mentioned the coincidence to Bob; he said that he painted it. Bob went inside the bus then returned and told us to come in. He introduced us to Charlie Manson. We bought some orange acid then wanted to leave. Bob said to come by the show at the Straight Theater later and ask for him.

We dropped the acid and I didn't want to drive back across the Bay so we went to the Straight Theater to hear some music. I asked for Bob at the door and he showed up with a revolver in holster on his side. Bob told us that they were recruiting some outsiders from the Four Square Church for ' The Process'. They looked like zombies waiting in line to give personal information, then get ID numbers tattooed on the inside of their lower lip. They were using one of those big pliers-like devices, like they use on livestock. It was a pretty weird image. We stayed next to one of the exits so we could leave; we didn't trust Bob but we were stoned and curious enough to stay.

We saw a guy we used to buy dope from while in line at different venues in the city. White Rabbit was always working lines at the Avalon, Fillmore or Family Dog and out at the Great Highway. He was working for the Straight Theater; we watched and talked for a few minutes. The music sucked it was unbearable on acid. We decided to leave out the side exit. I turned to look back and saw Bob in the street aiming the revolver at us. We ran several blocks to the Panhandle of Golden Gate Park at Masonic Avenue and then heard gunshots. We heard one more shot being fired when we were near Fell and Ashbury. We picked up my truck on Atalaya

Terrace, drove down Masonic and saw the police talking to Bob on the Panhandle down Fell Street.

If there is a connection between the cab driver killed by the Zodiac and Bob and Tom it could be that the cab driver lived at the exact area/and direction of the last gunshot and may have called the police and got Bob into trouble - a score that Bob would settle using Tom a few years later.

The next evening I went back to the black bus and bought more acid from Manson. While I was there, the SFPD TAC Squad made a Haight Street sweep from Masonic to Stanyan running everybody off or into Golden Gate Park. The door of the bus was open and they went past like it was invisible. Manson laughed, "God's eye watching."

At seventeen, I join the Military during the height of the Vietnam anti-war protests:

In January 1968, David Mullins and I decided to get out of Dodge by taking our chances in the Service. I joined the Army but Mullins was not able to because of a serious felony conviction on his record.

Bob, the CIA agent visits me at Boot Camp:

On February 28, 1968 through anti-war demonstration and a gauntlet of spitting protesters in front of the Oakland induction center (AFEES) I was sent to Fort Lewis Washington. A few weeks into basic training I received a message that I had a visitor - which was against regulations.

When I arrived at the Visitor Center an MP met me, "Who do you know in the CIA?" The MP questioned, "We just had someone show a CIA ID to the people here. This guy requested to see you. Do you know Robert Hemphill from Riverside, California?" I answered "no"; he went on to describe him as mid to late thirties, 5'9, 170 lbs, with dark hair. The MP asked, "What's up with this he flies up here causes an incident by landing at the airport with no approval or communication then comes to the visitor center to see you and disappears?"

In late May 1968 I graduated from Boot Camp and had
orders to report to Aberdeen Proving Grounds. I am
on the top row fourth from the right [below].

WOMAN IN THE
POLKA - DOT DRESS

L ate May 1968: While I was still home on leave I saw Bob in town at a triangular shaped parking lot in Sunol that we called the Bermuda Triangle because of its weird energy and strange occurrences. He stated to me, "I saw you talking to the pig". (He was referring to the MP at Fort Lewis.) I said, "He has your real name (a lie). You showed them a fake CIA ID." Bob responded, "I got news for them. It's real and we got something important going on. I don't have authorization to explain it to anyone."

Then I asked Bob if he killed his girlfriend. This had been nagging at me since the episode with his friend/relative on his driveway a year before. It was the first time it felt relatively safe bringing it up. Bob stated, "I don't use dope anymore and that's bullshit." He then said, "I have a big job down South in Los Angeles. I need a couple of people up here. You won't be breaking any laws just pick somebody up at the airport. Come to a meeting and I'll explain the details then." I was willing to cooperate because I was truly curious as I almost believed at this point that Bob was for real.

Later that afternoon I met Bob at his garage workshop; he was all dressed up in a dark suit and was wearing a light yellow-orange sweater. Around his neck was a chain with a decorative brass symbol. We got into his white 63' Chevy Biscayne and drove to North Livermore near the rifle range just a few miles from and in between the Lawrence Livermore Radiation Laboratory and the Alameda County Jail at Santa Rita.

I unwittingly re-visit the Santa Rita Safe House:

In a portion of North Livermore that appeared to be old military training area with outside parachute rigging tables and a rifle range located at opposite ends of the large tract of land and a big two-story house. The upstairs windows were boarded on three sides, the backside had windows... Three barns were set behind and thirty yards to each side of the house forming a triangle around a center barnyard. It was at the end of a 100- to 200- yard eucalyptus tree-lined driveway. The driveway continued through the barnyard and on through the center of the tract of land. There was a runway wind-sock and buildings that looked military or railroad; the dirt road continued a mile east and slightly south into a eucalyptus grove ending at what appeared to be an old church.

The church had several pews with double lightning bolts at the ends, a pulpit and altar with flags on either side. There were no pictures of Jesus or statues of any kind - it looked ceremonial not religious. Bob further stated. 'The purpose of the place originally was to build a militia; most were recruited former military people. But this place has always been a whorehouse."

RFK Assassination: The cast of characters:

When we drove back to the barnyard, there was an older black Cadillac parked near the house and a couple sitting in a gray primer Mustang that was parked closer to the barn at the north end of the barnyard.

Darlene Ferrin and Mike Mageau:

We parked near the middle of the yard between the house and the south barn and got out of the car. The girl and guy from the Mustang got out and walked over. The man (WMA) was approximately twenty years old, 5'10 - 6' in height and around one hundred and sixty-five lbs, with ruddy facial features. The woman (WFA) was attractive with a good curvy figure. She had a pug nose that was slightly crooked as if it had been broken at one time. She was in her twenties, approximately 5'4 in height and around one hundred and thirty lbs. with brown hair wearing a short skirt. She called Robert/Bob* (name used for this manuscript) Bobby other than that she seemed to know him well. For about five minutes they made small talk. I don't recall the specifics. She spoke to Bob; I just stood by observing it all. The other guy with her stood by as well. Bob was anticipating the arrival of somebody.

William J. Bryan MD:

A late model white Cadillac El Dorado pulled up into the yard and a WMA, very heavy set with brown, sandy colored hair and a beard got out. He was over 6', approximately mid to late forties years old, two hundred and seventy lbs. or bigger, and was wearing black rimmed glasses, Hawaiian shirt, white slacks and shoes.

Bob went over and talked quietly with him for a moment then went inside the house. The big man stepped over to us and said, "We are about to change the future of our nation and most of the world. We appreciate your willingness to participate." The girl appeared excited over this and seemed to know him as Doc.

Bob returned within a couple of minutes, walking out of the farmhouse with Tom and another man Tom was armed with a government model semi-auto 45 Caliber in holster and seemed to be guarding the WMA. He was Mexican or middle-eastern looking, approximately twenty-five years old, 5'4' and about one hundred and twenty lbs. with black hair wearing a T-shirt; khaki pants, and was barefoot. This guy looked sick, holding his stomach. He also had a bad intense chemical odor about him.

What emerged was a semi-circle of six of us facing toward the house and around the big bearded guy. The couple from the Mustang were the two at the northern part of the semicircle, Tom and the dazed, little barefoot guy who smelled like chemicals were the middle two, Bob was next and then I was at the south end. I was not facing the big bearded guy as much as facing toward the little dazed guy in the middle.

I kept staring waiting for him to focus on someone, the pretty girl, the big guy in front of him, Tom, anyone or anything, but he never did. Bob introduced the big bearded guy in the Hawaiian shirt to me as Dr. William J. Bryan. Bob, Tom and the girl seemed to already know him. I don't recall the reaction of the guy escorting the girl and the little barefoot guy was so dazed he wouldn't have comprehended anything. I had the strange impression that this meeting was mostly for my benefit but I was not exactly sure why.

Bryan went on with words to the effect:

"This could be our final chance before the election and the Antichrist continues on course to Armageddon. Evil will dominate the world and millions will suffer and die. Let us act now to stop his unfortunate curse, let us change this cycle in history at Los Angeles for the World."

Bob separated me from the group and took me to the south barn at gunpoint. I was completely overcome by fear. Not the fear of being held at gunpoint but a deeper fear of powerlessness conjured up from within me by something familiar about the place. The gun had only triggered it and I was terrified. Inside the barn, I saw there was a chair with five point restraints and some kind of head apparatus. Other medical equipment was stored off to one side. I presumed this was for use in the farmhouse where the dazed little guy had come from but I didn't really know. I don't know what happened to me shortly after this, and if that while I was under I was filmed, but there was professional film equipment set up in the barn flood lights, a large tripod and professional grade movie camera. I was still at gunpoint when Bob directed me to take a tin can that was set on one of the framing members of the barn wall near the entry. It had a foul-smelling liquid in it. Bob forced me to drink what he described as dog piss and strychnine from the tin can. I immediately began choking until I blacked out. I am uncertain how long I was totally unconscious I next recall riding with Tom in Bob's white Chevy then being dumped off at San Francisco International Airport. I boarded a flight to Dulles Airport in Virginia and reported for duty at Aberdeen Proving Grounds in Maryland.

Robert F. Kennedy is assassinated in Los Angeles June 4, 1968: Robert F. Kennedy reportedly spent his final day at the Malibu Beach house of John Frankenheimer, the director of the 1962 film 'Manchurian Candidate'. (Compounding the morbid irony of RFK spending his last evening with his friend the director of Manchurian Candidate, William J. Bryan MD, the hypnosis expert, and self-described Director of Air Force Medical

Survival was a technical consultant to the film.) Just after midnight Senator Kennedy who had just won the California Primary in his effort to secure the Democratic nomination was shot in the pantry of the Ambassador Hotel on Wilshire Boulevard in Los Angeles.

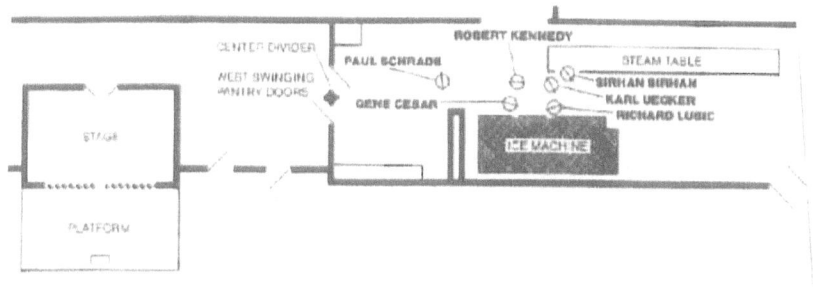

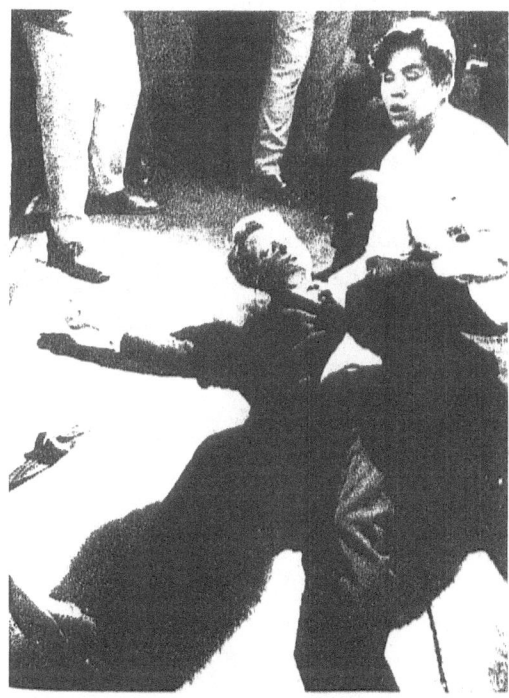

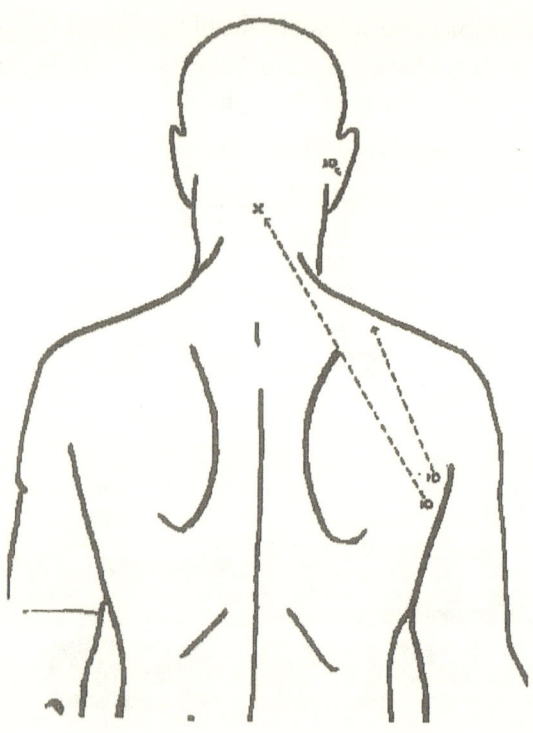

LAPD bullet trajectory diagram

Excerpted from the Vallejo Times Herald June 6, 1968

June 6, 1968: Vallejo and Los Angeles Police Departments were
investigating accusations that a Vallejo woman was involved
in the shooting of Kennedy – possibly the girl in the polka
dot dress. The accuser, according to the Vallejo Times
Herald, was an anonymous woman neighbor. "The officer
said that he received a telephone call from a woman who
suggested that 'my neighbor might have been mixed up in
that shooting down south.' But, the officer said, the woman
who called would not give either her name or address, or
the name of the woman she was accusing."

Numerous eye-witness reports of Kennedy's assassination described a
young woman in a polka-dot dress who. The woman was described as a
Caucasian 23-27, 5'6", wearing a polka-dot dress, dark shoes, and bouffant-

type brunette hair. Later the Vallejo Herald times reported that the Los Angeles Police Department was investigating reports that a Vallejo woman was involved in the shooting possibly the girl in the polka dotted dress. She was seen leaving the scene with a man......

Suggestions of cover-up: June 6, 1968: Los Angeles Police Department Crime Lab test fired an Iver Johnson Cadet model .22 caliber revolver serial number H18602 and confirmed it as the murder weapon. Revolver number H53725 was the gun purchased by Sirhan and taken from him at the pantry of the Ambassador Hotel by witnesses and held. California State records reveal that Iver Johnson Cadet Model .22 caliber revolver serial number H18602 was destroyed. Reason No wants.

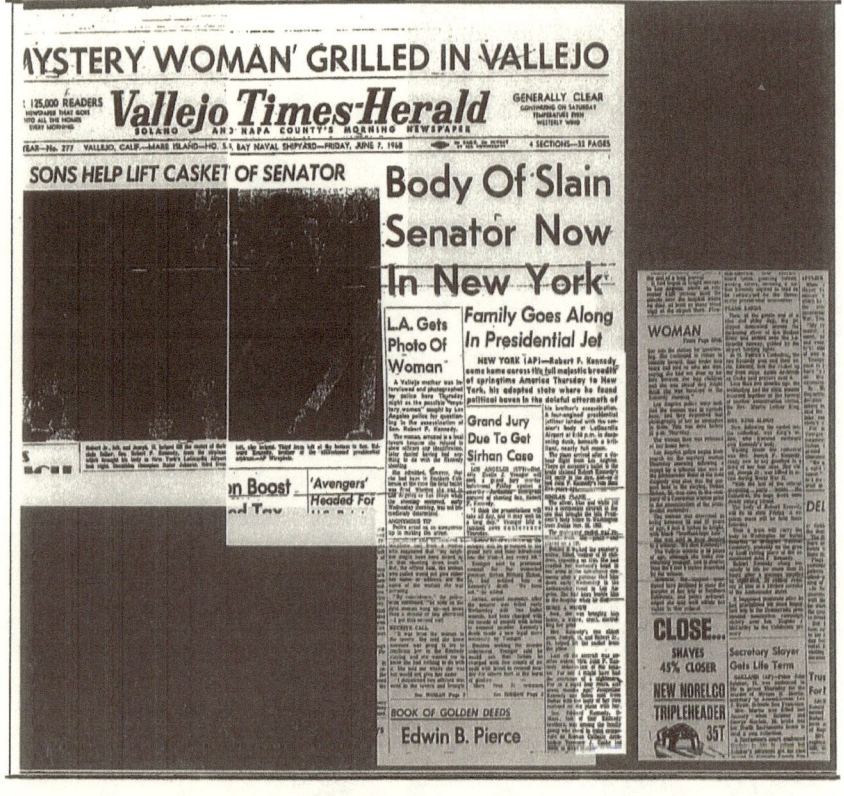

Darlene Ferrin, Vallejo, CA
1969 Police Report/Zodiac Victim 3:
The WFA was identified as Darlene
Elizabeth FERRIN, 1300 Virginia St.
Blonde, 5'4", 128, dob 3-17-47

Eyewitness descriptions of 'Polka-dot Dress Girl' seen accompanying Sirhan, and yelling "We shot him" following the RFK's assassination:

- Prior to the shooting, suspect observed with a female cauc., 23/27, 5-6, wearing a white voile dress, ¾ inch sleeves, with small black polka dots, dark shoes, bouffant type hair. This female not identified or in custody.

- Serrano: thought the girl was between the ages of 23 and 27, with her hair not quite coming to her shoulders, done in a "bouffant" style, wearing a polka dot dress with a bib collar and ¾ length sleeves. She also recalled that the girl had a "funny" nose.

- Seim—who, like Serrano, DiPierro and Hanson, had noticed the girl's 'funny nose'—... "She was very persistent," he told the police. He thought the girl's nose might have been broken at one time, and described her as Caucasian but with an olive complexion.

- DiPierro: "...she looked as though she was sick." He described her as Caucasian and as about 20 or 21 years old, definitely no older than 24. She was "very shapely" and was wearing a "white dress with—it looked like either black or dark violet polka dots on it and kind of a [bib-like] collar." He said her hair color was "Brown, I would say brunette," "puffed up a little" and that it came to just above her shoulders. DiPierro told the FBI that she had a peculiar-looking nose.

- Karen Ross described her to the LAPD as having a nose that had been "maybe fixed", a white dress with black polka dots, ¾ length sleeves, dark blond hair worn in a "puff" and with a round face.

- Eve Hansen had talked to a girl in a white dress with black or navy blue polka dots approximately the size of a quarter who had dark brown hair that hung just above the shoulders, who had a "turned-up nose".

- Dr. Marcus McBroom was in the pantry behind Elizabeth Evans, one of the shooting victims. He exited the kitchen through the double doors at the West end and noticed a brunette woman aged 20-26, medium build, "wearing a white dress with silver dollar size polka dots

- Jeanette Prudhomme also saw two men, one of which looked like Sirhan and the other of which was wearing a gold shirt, in the company of a woman who appeared to be 28-30, with brown, shoulder length hair, wearing a white dress with black polka dots.

The following is directly from the RFK case files...

June 5, 1968 LAPD case # 68-5731 (Polka Dot Dress Investigation)- Corroborated allegations:

At 4:25a.m at Parker Center, investigators interviewed Vincent Di Pierro. During this interview Di Pierro stated that he is employed at the Ambassador Hotel as a waiter. He stated that he was in the pantry when Senator Kennedy was shot and that he observed the shooting. He saw Sirhan on at tray stand in the pantry area at the east end of the ice machine. He observed a female wearing a polka dot dress standing next to Sirhan.

INTERROGATED BY: Sergeant F.J. Pachett # 7872, Rampart Detectives.

Sergeant A.B Melendres #3214, Rampart Detectives.

John E Howard, District Attorney

George Murphy, Bureau of Investigation

By Sergeant Pachett:

Q-And then as the Senator walked toward this man, somebody got in front of him?

By Mr. Di Peirro:

A-Yes, these, you know, the people all mingles in this one area and he pushed his way through. The only reason that he was noticeable was because there was this good-looking girl in the crowd there.

Q-All right, was the girl with him?

A-It looked as though, yes

Q-What makes you say that?

A-Well she was following him.

Q-Where did she follow him?

A-From – she was standing behind the tray stand because she was up next to him on – behind, and she was holding on to the other end of the tray table and she like- it looked like as if she was almost holding him.

Q-Did you see him get off the straight stand?

A-Yes, I did

Q-And then he walked toward the Senator?

A-Yes

Q-This girl,-

A-She stayed there.

Q-At the tray stand?

A-Right, I glanced over once in a while, she was good-looking so I looked at her.

Q-What is it in your mind that makes you think they were together, the fact that they were standing together?

A-No, no, he turned when he was on the tray stand once and he had the same stupid smile on, you know, and then he kind of turned and said something. I don't know what he said.

By Mr. Howard:

Q-You did see him speak to her?

A-He turned as though he did say something, whether he said anything-

Q-Did she move her mouth like she was speaking to him?

A-No, she just smiled

Q-But in other words, he was looking towards, say, the Senator?

A-Yes, He was holding on up here and there was another pole behind him, where she was holding on and he turned like this, as though to say something, and whether his lips moved or not I couldn't see that.

Q-And it was after he turned and she smiled?

A-She smiled

Q-And would it seem to you that she smiled at something that had been said?

A-Yeah, or-

Q-or that she was smiling because the Senator was walking towards her?

A-No, when she first entered she looked as though she was sick also.

Q-All right, this girl, what nationality would you say she was? Any idea at all?

A-No, all I know is she was white.

Q-She was white; Caucasian?

A-Yes, a Caucasian girl.

Q-What is the youngest this girl could be?

A-21,20,21.

Q-At least 20 or 21?

A-Yes

Q-Would you have no question about serving her a drink in a bar?

A-Oh no, no.

Q-She was definitely of age?

A-Yes.

Q-What is the oldest you think she was?

A-I don't know, about 24.

Q-All right, how tall was this girl?

A-I really couldn't determine because I only saw her in the dining room. I never saw her standing on the ground.

Q-In relation to the fellow who was standing on the tray thing that we discussed, that was four inches above the ground, where was her head in relation to his body; were they about the same height at that time or-

A-You could say approximately.

Q-Well, when they turned to talk to her-

A-They were almost eye level.

Q-They were almost eye level at this time?

A-But, you see with the tray stand you would never know how it's balanced. I don't know whether one end was higher because the way it is now, its central, its not equalized.

Q-so, you couldn't really –

A-You cant really judge, no.

Q-How about her build, could you see it?

A-Oh, yeah.

Q-Oh yeah, What does that mean?

A-Very sharply

Q-She wasn't skinny, she wasn't fat?

A-No

Q-What was the girl wearing?

A-She had a white dress with- it looked like black or dark violet polka dots on it and kind of bively (phonetic) collar.

Q-A what kind of collar?

A-A thing that goes around like that. I don't know what they call it.

By Mr. Howard

Q-Pretty greasy looking?

A-You could go out- you couldn't go the Coconut Grove with it, you know, but it was a nice dress to dress up in, a nice dress.

By Sergeant Pachett:

Q-How about this girl's hair, what color was it?

A-Brown, I would say a brunette.

Q-Your hair is brown

A-Yes

Q-Lighter or darker then yours

A-little darker than mine

Q-Was it long or short or what?

A-I would say about to here, not much longer

Q-Just above the shoulders

A-Just above the shoulders kind of-

By Sergeant Melenderes:

Q-To her neck?

A-Yes, about the neck, maybe just a little longer, I don't know.

By Sergeant Pachett:

Q-Was it straight or curly?

A-One side was a little puffed up a little.

Q-Did you see anyone else with this girl that you recall?

A-Not that I recall. Those were the only two people I saw on the tray stand.

Q-All right, did you see this girl after the shootin?

A-No, I was too busy trying to see what I could do.

Q-Do you recall seeing her during the shooting?

A-No, I just saw the girl and I forgot about her and everything else but the gun.

June 5, 1968 11:30am Los Angeles Police Department broadcast on APB Emergency Tele-type requesting information for the arrest of a women in the polka dot dress. The description was as follows:

"Female Caucasian, 23-27, 5-6, wearing a white violet dress, ¾ sleeves with small black polka dots, dark shoes, bouffant-type hair."

June 6, 1969 Booker Griffin also at the Ambassador Hotel during the evening and night of the shooting-he witnessed the following:

"The man that did the shooting was in the corridor-way as I left in advance of the Senator. He was there with a tall Caucasian male and a Caucasian female in a white dress. I noticed the man because I had seen him first downstairs in the Ambassador Room around 10:15pm. I remember distinctly because we had stared each other down. I vaguely remember the girl also with him. Between 11 and the actual shooting, I travelled between the Embassy Room and the pressroom (using the corridor where the incident occurred) maybe six or eight times. The last three or four times I noticed the gunman, the girl and the other guy.

When I left the stage and went to the pressroom the last time before the shooting, there were a few kitchen employees and the gunman and his two friends. I distinctly remember this because the gunman had sneered at me as I went past. This affected me to the point that it stayed on my mind when I sat down in the pressroom. I made a remark to some friends in the pressroom about the guy and how we just seemed to dislike each other, it puzzled me. I extended greetings to Bud Schulberg and his wife Geri and was leaving the pressroom to peep the corridor when the shooting occurred. I was just stepping out the door when the first shot was fired. I had a full view of the whole room. I differ very sharply with media reports at this point. I distinctly saw the other man and the girl flee a side corridor heading out of the Hotel as I raced to the feet of the fallen Senator. There is no doubt in my mind that on several trips past the trio that they were together.

I tried to get through to pursue them down the corridor, but couldn't get through. I was pushed and shoved by newsmen and Kennedy staff. I kept yelling they're getting away.

WILLIAM TURNER (Former FBI Special Agent and author):

"Only hours after the RFK shooting and before Sirhan had been identified, Dr. Brian appeared on the Los Angeles radio program of Ray Briem (KABC) and offhandedly commented that the suspect probably acted under posthypnotic suggestion."

JAY ROBERT NASH (Author)

"Sirhan Sirhan was sitting in police headquarters joking with his guards while Kennedy slipped deeper into death. "You are lazy man" he said John Howard deputy district attory, "You should exercise." Before, a sergeant handed him a cup of coffee. The murderer jokingly asked him to sample it. The officer did. "If anything happens," the sergeant said, "we both go together." Sirhan laughed, "I'll hold you to that."The sergeant, W. C. Johnson, somehow got drawn into a discussion with Sirhan concerning the Boston Stranger.

The police sergeant explained how the killer made a fancy bow out of a stocking he used to strangling his victims. "That's real cruel." Sirhan Bishara Sirhan said solemnly. " I wonder often what would cause a man to do such a thing."

Sept 28, 1975: Dr. Edward Simson-Kallas, psychologist and hypnosis expert who conducted tests on Sirhan in San Quentin prison in 1969 has stated that Sirhan was a kind of "Manchurian Candidate" hypno-programmed to shoot Senator Kennedy.

"He (Sirhan) was easily influenced, had no real roots and was looking for casue. The Arab-Israeli conflict could easily have been used to motivate him. He was hypnotized by someone."

"Sirhan could not be trusted to kill Kennedy alone. He's always been a loser. He failed at Pasadena City College. He played the horses and lost. He wanted to be a jockey and he fell off a horse. He was the perfect subject for programming as a scapegoat. I see him as an excellent follower, willing to risk his life for an idea….not afraid of death. Basically, he is a moral person. Sirhan was ideal for the role because he had not been in this country long enough to establish any self-identification."

Other murders Simson had interviewed spoke with great expression and detail of their crimes. Sirhan, though, spoke as though he were "reciting from a book." " He said 'Yes I killed Kennedy. I did it to help the Arabs. I did it to help the Arab refugees."

"He seemed to take joy in assuming the role of an Arab hero. The curious thing was that he didn't have any details. A psychologist always looks for details. If a person is involved in a real situation, there are details..."

In later interviews, as Sirhan began to trust the psychologist, he changed the way he talked about the crime. "He seemed very concerned, asking me to hypnotize him to find out what really happened. 'I don't really know what happened. I know I was there, they tell me I killed Kennedy. I don't remember what exactly I did but I know I wasn't myself. I remember there was a girl who wanted coffee. She wanted coffee with lots of cream and sugar. So I gave her my cup and poured one for myself. That's the last I can remember until I was choked and manhandled by the crowd.'

Human Engineering Laboratory

I am on duty at Aberdeen Proving Grounds Aberdeen in Maryland. I tell them my story:

I saw the front-page picture of the guard's clip-on tie sprawled on the floor (I found out later missing from Gene Cesar's neck) next to RFK. I was physically ill when I went to the Provost Marshall's office to tell them what I knew about the meeting at Santa Rita farm in North Livermore. I was on 'casual status' taking tests, like the Minnesota Multiphasic Personality Inventory (three times), and EEG tests to measure psychological response during polygraph interrogation sessions at CIA Human Engineering Laboratory on Aberdeen Proving Grounds. They caught me randomly marking M.M.P.I. answer sheets like a moron (randomly). They were going to kill me but instead they changed my status to 'Special Purpose'. I reported directly to HEL.

Every day I cleaned monkey cages and fed monkeys with wires coming out of the top of their heads like the little girl in North Livermore. They were kept in boxes with only their heads exposed so they couldn't touch the wires. I had to feed them bananas one at a time and give them water. Some days I would be put in isolation for hours and sometimes just taking tests... One day in an interrogation interview they told me that they had been exposing my balls to radiation by a device in the chair. They told me that I would die of cancer in a few years. They asked my thought on this. I told the Dr. that if I find out that its true I would come back to kill him.

Later that day I spoke with a Federal agent named Malcolm Baldridge from Washington D.C. He asked me to describe the old church adjacent to the Santa Rita farm. When I mentioned double lightning bolts on the pews he smiled and stared for a long while. He had a CIA file on me that he read from, and then said, "I know the Bay Area well and I have good friends there like the Roddy family." I also knew the family; Bonnie Roddy had been my childhood sweetheart.

He asked if I would let them hypnotize me. I agreed and when they put me under I began suffocating just like I did in the barn after being forced to drink the poison. When I was able to speak, my voice sounded like that of a little girl. This was all documented on film at Aberdeen Proving Grounds. Years later, a friend saw a segment of the film showing me being hypnotized at a showing in Berkeley, CA.

Bob threatens me at Aberdeen:

I received a call from Hemphill at my barracks. He stated that he would kill my parents if I didn't meet him at the railroad station in Aberdeen. He also insisted that I wear my uniform and further stated, 'There is somebody important that I want you to meet. "I agreed to meet them the next day.

That evening I couldn't sleep and went to the Enlisted Men's Club. I would find out later the club was actually part of the Limited War Laboratory' at HEL. I had a few drinks and without warning someone started firing shots inside the club. I heard the hammer hit, saw the flash, tasted and smelled the smoke, it was just behind me. More shots were fired outside and I ran all the way back to the barracks. I felt strange body sensations like I was coming onto some acid. It progressed with no hallucinations, just a lot of unpleasant body feeling with no paranoia, it was like mescaline. That was the strangest part of this. I ran to get away but felt no fear.

The next day I felt the drug:

I showered while smoking a cigar and I was stuck. I knew that Bob had explicitly requested that I wear my uniform. I also sensed that I was being set up for something, yet I knew that if I declined, one of my loved ones may have to pay for my choice. I tried to figure the best way out of it. I came up with the idea of just doing a bad job of complying intuitive form of zig-zag Zen.

I would try but screw up. That way I may be spared my fate by their frustration with my incompetence. I decided to show up at the train station as agreed, but to wear civilian clothes instead of my uniform. I went by bus to the railroad. I got off the bus and soon saw Bob in the parking lot behind the station, he was yelling at me for not wearing my uniform. As I approached Bob: Tom, dressed in military fatigues, came running toward me from the station with a knife in his hand. Afraid that he was trying to stab me, I kicked him in the stomach, grabbed the knife out of his hand then tossed him to the pavement.

A woman started screaming and we ran in different directions. I caught a cab to get back to Aberdeen Proving Grounds and we got pulled over by the Aberdeen Police. I had blood on my nose from the scuffle with Tom. The police questioned me for several hours about what happened at the station. They checked my hands for glue, they found none, and then accused me of being under the influence of drugs and released me. Tom was caught running down the street and arrested. I was shocked to find that none of this was in the local papers. I felt the unpleasant effects of the drug for days and I was sure it wasn't EA-1729 or 'PI'. I know this because I tried stolen CIA Acid recreationally and it was good!

In retrospect, I believe that Tom must have done something to somebody at the train station with the knife and then intended to frame me with it to get me out of the way while the RFK assassination investigation was still so hot.

Bob stalks my girlfriend:

I asked my father to wire some money so I could come home for three days because my girlfriend, Claudine Anderson, and her sister Sandy were scared. I wanted to be home on Halloween. Bob was stalking them and when they called the Alameda County Sheriff's Department nothing was done. He continued to 'check on her'. Nothing happened and I returned to Aberdeen Proving Grounds and completed a counter-insurgency course.

HEL hypnotizes one hundred including me. October 29, 1968:

I also participated in a significant experiment the mass hypnotism of more than one hundred soldiers at once. This experiment lasted more than one hour with no recall, no memory of what we were told or programmed to do. The group hypnotism was followed up with isolation and polygraph interrogation sessions at Human Engineering Laboratory.

The Zodiac killings begin to unfold:

December 15, 1968: I flew to New Jersey and reported to Fort Dix for overseas transport to West Germany. I was assigned to the 122nd Ordinance Battalion 3rd Armor Division at Hanau near Frankfurt. A couple days after my arrival I received a letter from Bob Hemphill. "I will be over to see you about another job". He signed it with a Z and it was folded over like a card with 'Happy Christmas' on the front.

December 20, 1968: Two teenagers on their first date, David Faraday and Betty Lou Jensen are shot to death in a parked car out in the ranchlands on Lake Herman Road outside Vallejo, California.

January 1969: I was interviewed in Frankfurt by two FBI agents and gave a statement concerning the railroad station incident in Aberdeen Maryland. I was told Tom was still being held and it was possible that I could be sent back to testify or even face charges myself.

Russians invaded the Czech Republic and we were on red alert because of the build-up of Russian tanks on the Czech-West German border. Part of my unit would be sent to the border. Thinking this could make it difficult for Hemphill to locate me, I volunteered.

Supplier Of Arms For The Westcoast Avengers

Bob shows up in Germany:

February 1969: (Hanau, Germany) I returned from the field to hear stories about a friend of mine recruiting mercenaries. Bob was again using the name Bob Hemphill I got up sick in the morning and headed to the PX to get something for my stomach when I saw Bob near the barbershop. He said "Come on you need a haircut." He was smoking a lot more, one after another. I noticed this because he once told me that he used to get serious headaches and could only smoke a little pot at night. He complained about being detained at Roth Air Force Base for days.

He insisted that I go to the John Wayne movie to talk with him then he would leave my girlfriend alone. That evening we met at the theater. I wanted to talk about what happened at the meeting in North Livermore and the railroad station in Aberdeen Maryland.He acted like he couldn't hear me and spoke about another big job. Bob said, "What the fuck, if you weren't born into this you would have been dead a long time ago." I felt that everyone in the theater was staring at us. "This job will require several people and we need guns: M-14s, (automatic assault rifles), M79s (grenade launchers) and one M-60 (belt fed machine gun)." I laughed and said, "How am I supposed to get them?" Bob said, "We will put you in charge of them. I'll be back. Want me to say anything to your girlfriend?"He stood up as the credits were running and recited poetry, "He plunged himself into the billowy wave, and echo arose from the suicides grave, titwillow, titwillow." I walked away and didn't look back.

February 21, 1969: LAPD Sergeant Phil Sartuche investigating the assassination reportedly flew north to the Livermore Valley.

During a brief R&R at the Green Arrow Hotel in Garmisch West Germany an individual in the casino asked to speak with me concerning the RFK assassination and murderers in the Bay Area. He told me that he was from San Francisco and was writing a book.

I was afraid to speak:

I had feelings of hopelessness at this point and assumed he wouldn't believe me anyway. It would just get family members and friends killed. I self medicated myself into a stupor and less than a week later I am back in Hanau. I received special reassignment orders from Sergeant Robert Bigley, my platoon leader. Bigley informed me that I would be in charge of maintaining an 'armament float' (weapons for issue, replacement or special assignments).

Bigley further stated, "You start Monday by picking up some heavy barrel match grade M-14s in Hanau." I felt the same terror building up - who would believe any of this now. I arrived in Hanau and reported to the Armament Section (depot echelon). Personnel there treated me as though I had some kind of rank. A quarter ton truck pulled up and the driver asked me to meet him the secured area.

I asked a Spec 5 what was going on. He stated, "I really don't care what you do with the guns after you sign for them." He asked for my ID and I signed for the weapons then we loaded them into the truck. We drove toward Frankfurt to a place in the country with high stonewalls. Once inside, I could see that it was a range with firing positions and a range master's tower. There were individuals wearing fatigues with berets, Bob was lecturing them.

He was dressed in fatigue pants, a brown leather jacket and wearing the black ball cap with the red goat head. He walked over to me and said, "Act professional damn it, this is important." I asked him what was going on, "You'll read about it in the papers asshole." He called some of the individuals over to unload the rifles then said, "Don't worry I'll keep your girlfriend happy."

I did read about this in the papers, the group of mercenaries headed to fight in the Haitian revolution to assassinate Francois 'Papa Doc' Duvalier, but their 70-foot boat sunk in a storm just off the coast. Reportedly, the B-26 attack bomber piloted by a CIA contract employee. He made the bombing run on the palace.

May 19, 1969: I received Special Orders Number 139 from the Department of the Army Headquarters 3rd Armored Division. I was ordered to depart West Germany and report to Fort Lewis Washington. After thirty days, I would leave for additional training and transport to Vietnam.

```
                         DEPARTMENT OF THE ARMY
                  HEADQUARTERS, 3D ARMORED DIVISION
                             APO 09039

SPECIAL ORDERS                                              19 May 1969
NUMBER   139                        EXTRACT

44.  TC 249.  Fol rsg dir eff on EDCSA.  Indiv will rept as indic for trans to
CONUS enr to new asg.  Indiv will rept to CONUS trans area at the hour on the
date specified in PC for trans to new asg.  WP. TDY TPA in CONUS.

Fol info applies to indiv as indic:
Rept to:  Bldg 110 FAPOE Rhein/Main AB Frankfurt, FRG NLT 0200 hrs on 22 May 69
Asg to:  USA OS Repl Sta Ft Lewis WA for fur asg to unit indic below.
PC data:  Rept to USA OS Repl Sta Ft Lewis WA NLT 29 Jun 69 for VN POR Tng
Auth:  DA Ltr, subj: E6 & Below OS Vol asg & progress instr fr EPADR-CAV
       dtd 31 Mar 69
PCS (MDC):  ZXEO     Lv data:  30 DDALV     VRB dsg:  NA
EM Mail adrs:  Pers Mail Section, APO SF CA 96381

SILVEY, DAVID M RA67284583 ███████████ PFC 45B20 HQ & Co A 122d Maint Bn
W&FATOA APO NY 09165
For fur asg to:  USARV Trans Det APO SF CA 96384
Temp adrs:  PO Box 103 Sunol, CA
OPO C&L No:  VQG 9313     PPSC:  C     ETS:  28 Feb 71
BASD&BPED:  29 Feb 68     EDCSA:  24 May 69
Tvl data:  WBI this HQ, PMB UFREC of PC.  AMD FRF-WRI-3PC-3300-AZ-5
           (CIC 2 9 1 A 03)  Flt#T234
           APOD:  McGuire AFB Wrightstown, NJ

Fol info applies to above indivs:
Sp instr:  Proc rqr by USAREUR Reg 614-50 WB compl prior to dprt.  DA Form 2142,
    Request for Pay Action, for partial/advance or advance tvl payment, if auth
    and desired WB forwarded so as to arrive this HQ ATTN: AETFFO ASAP for short-
    notice departures or NLT 10 days prior to departure for normal redeployments.
    Indiv will rept for payment NLT 3 working days prior to PC date.  A compl DA
    Form 2166, Enl Effcy Rept, placed in a sealed envelope, will accompany EM rept
    to this HQ for outproc.  Plague imm rqr for tvl to or through Vietnam.  Tvl
    need not be delayed except for 1st vaccine dose.  Indiv WB given the malaria
    con indoc prior to dprt fr home sta.  Upon arr at POE indiv will have in his
    poss only those items spec in Appendix IV, AR 700-8400-1, as changed.  EM
    scheduled for VN orientation at Ft Lewis WA will have in his poss 1 pr leather
    gloves w/2 pr wool liners.  Upon compl of orientation indiv wil send gloves
    to HOR or place of residence or surr them for non-temp Govt storage.  EM must
    arr in Vietnam wearing khaki trousers & short sleeved shirt or tropical fatigue
    Tropical fatigues WBI to auth indiv at POE.  Cncr tvl of depn, shpmt of HHG
    & POV to Vietnam not auth.  Indiv auth to wear summer civ clothing in Vietnam.
    In the event PC Instr have not been rec at least 10 days prior to avel date
    spec in your orders, rept to the nearest mil inst to obtain assistance in
    ascertaining the status of your PC by calling Western Area MTMTS Oakland CA
    (AUTOVON 831-1900 or Area Code 415 466-2802).  Auth is granted to call collect
    by comml telephone if circumstances prevent your contacting or rept to the
    nearest mil inst.  In either case, if PC Instr are not obtained, you are dir
    to rept to USA OS Repl Sta Ft Lewis WA NLT 1200 hrs 29 Jun 69.  Any add time
```

Para 44 SO 139 DA HQ 3d Armd Div APO 09039 dtd 19 May 69 (cont)

nec to cover the period bwtn the available or rept date spec in this order & the rept date spec in the PC is auth as DDALV. Wear of the Army Green uniform is rqr for indiv tvl in uniform in CONUS during the winter season. Alcoholic bev NTE 1 US Gal (per mbr of family 21 yrs or older if depn accomp indiv) auth dy free entry into CONUS. EM auth bag alw of 66 lbs w/134 lbs excess for air tvl.

FOR THE COMMANDER:

OFFICIAL:

JOHN W. VESSEY JR.
Colonel, GS
Chief of Staff

GLEN M. HEWITT
2LT, AGC
Asst AG

DISTRIBUTION:
30-Indiv conc; 10-Indiv 201 file; 3-AETFAG-FMB, AETFFO; 2-AETFAG-ASD; 1-PSNCO
5-AETFAG-FRB Reports Unit, USA OS Repl Sta Ft Lewis WA
5-VN Trans Det APO SF CA 96384; 5-122d Maint Bn; 1-Redeployment, AMB Analyst

THE PAINTING PARTY

I arrived back in Sunol early Saturday afternoon on May 24, 1969:

My friend picked me up at the airport and spoke of a property that he was going to that evening in Vallejo with Bob Hemphill. I declined; we partied together up until Bob arrived to pick him up. Bob appeared more humble or depressed about his recent failure. I asked him what happened in Haiti. Bob stared at the ground; he asked if I could get some reds and cross-tops. I refused. He then said, "They're not for me; it's for a friend of mine. She knows about you and is having a party. There will be a lot of women at the party and it's going to be wild. You deal to her directly the jars I've been getting from you guys have been going to her for a couple of years." We got into his white 63' Chevy Biscayne that was still registered to my friend and went down Kilkare Canyon to Dave Mullin's house and picked up two jars of cross-tops. We continued on to Vallejo to what turned out to be a small family-type painting party at 1300 Virginia Street, the home of Darlene Ferrin.

Darlene Ferrin and Mike Mageau:

May 24, 1969: I remember that Darlene Ferrin's sister Pam was sitting near the front door like a security guard that evening. I was wearing Levi's and a blue shirt, my friend was wearing just about the same. Bob was all dressed up, wearing a light, almost-orange sweater and dark sport coat. I was both disappointed when we saw that it was a family-type thing. I remember a lady with her hair rolled up, she was running the party, but nobody was painting. We just kind of stood there like bumps on a log then I noticed Pam was sitting in the middle of the couch between Mike Mageau and some other guy. I had some hash and some orange mescaline that I offered to them. The lady saw what was happening and got upset because Pam was pregnant & then Pam's brother got involved. Darlene came out of the kitchen with Bob (arguing) and I was shocked to then recognize her as being the girl at the meeting at Santa Rita farm in North Livermore. At this point it occurred to me that Mike was probably also there. We went into the kitchen and I sold her the two jars as Bob continued to harass her with, "Bryan can make you crazy; make you kill that baby!"

Darlene put the jars in an empty baby bottle and placed it behind full bottles in the refrigerator, then begged Bob to leave her alone. We talked; I asked her if we could smoke some hash. She said the only place was the bedroom or in the back, but that was a problem right now. Pam came into the kitchen and I could hear her brother still bad-mouthing us in the living room so I went back to see what the problem was. I remember he was wearing a black vest and had tattoos on his arms.

Darlene said that he was really not a bad guy just has a big mouth. I wanted to talk to her about what happened in Livermore. It didn't seem like that was going to happen so my friend and I decided to leave, but Bob stayed. Pam was back at the front door and I told her that I hoped to see her again. Sadly, I never had the opportunity. From the front yard I turned and waved goodbye to her. As we walked toward the street I noticed that a white Cadillac parked in front and Dr. Bryan, wearing a suit, making his way along the house. I stopped long enough to make eye contact and noticed that Bryan looked concerned. Then my friend and I hitchhiked back to Sunol.

Bob reveals story behind Crash of Pacific Airlines Flight #773 (Reference to Chapter 1):

According to him 'Grand Chingon' William J. Bryan who was legendary to 'insiders; famous for his monstrous deeds in circles of ultimate evil. Bob often boasted in bits and pieces on helping Bryan, who was a former airline pilot brainwash a Philippine national - Francisco Gonzales.

Hemphill stated that they recruited Gonzales in San Francisco with filmed adolescent sex then used blackmail to help program him with poison and hypnosis at Santa Rita farm. Bob told me that Gonzales was prepared by

Bryan to crash a Reno-to-San Francisco bound commercial airliner into a satellite tracking station. Gonzales was drugged while at the Palace Hotel in Reno then after a stop in Stockton was triggered when the plane started to descend near the North Livermore Valley. According to the accident report, investigators discovered that Gonzales had advised both friends and relatives that he would die either on Wednesday May 6th, or Thursday, May 7th.He referred to his impending death on a daily basis throughout the week preceding the incident.

When the Fairchild F-27A (N2770R) with 43 other people started to descend over the safe house and mysterious ground-based wire antennae - Gonzales, fully triggered, pulled out his gun, entered the cockpit and shot the pilot Ernest Clark. At 6:48 p.m. the aircraft radioed its last message, First Officer Raymond Andress was heard saying, 'Skipper's shot. We've been shot. Trying to help.' Pacific Airlines Flight #773 actually flew over Santa Rita farm and crashed into the side of a hill near San Ramon. Bob suggested the whole terrifying tragedy was filmed from the safe house. "We film everything".

One of the forty four people killed was San Francisco Police Inspector George F. Lacau. According to Hemphill, Bryan harbored a deep-rooted hatred for the SFPD and Lacau personally, because of an argument that took place in the bar at the Waterfront Restaurant. According to Bob, they had to close the safe house at 225 Chestnut Street in San Francisco's North Beach because of local heat concerning crime and complaints about reported adolescent prostitution. Hemphill further stated that, days after the National Guard left the crash site, Bryan celebrated evil with a black mass. Bob made sure that we knew that they could do this to anyone! Bob harassed Darlene at the painting party the same way. "Bryan can make you do anything; make you kill that baby!" This was followed up with the unexpected arrival and personal appearance of Dr. Bryan for leverage.

A few days later I saw my friend Bob Ussery who was home in Sunol after being wounded in Vietnam. Bob was in some ways like my father strong and honest. I told Bob that Hemphill was some kind of killer fag. Bob replied, "Maybe little kids, he used to make me sick when he would talk about killing kids. He was always trying to get me to write stuff for him in trade for his working on my car at the gas station where he worked."

Bob said Hemphill couldn't read or write. Bob Ussery owned a light blue 55' Chevy four-door and a 56'Ford.

June 29, 1969: I caught a flight from San Francisco to Seattle, completed several days survival counter-insurgency training at Fort Lewis Washington then departed for Vietnam from McCord Air Force Base, also in Washington.

We stopped in Guam to refuel we got out and walked around for about 2 hours. It was warm here at night with a lot of bugs and lizards around. At this point everyone looked nervous as we got back on the plane.

July 4, 1969: Just before midnight I looked out the window of the plane down to see explosions and fires burning everywhere on the ground. For the first time in what seemed along time I actually felt safe. I felt like I could sleep and live without apprehension away from the gang stalking manipulation and control. We arrived at Cam Ran Bay Republic of Vietnam.

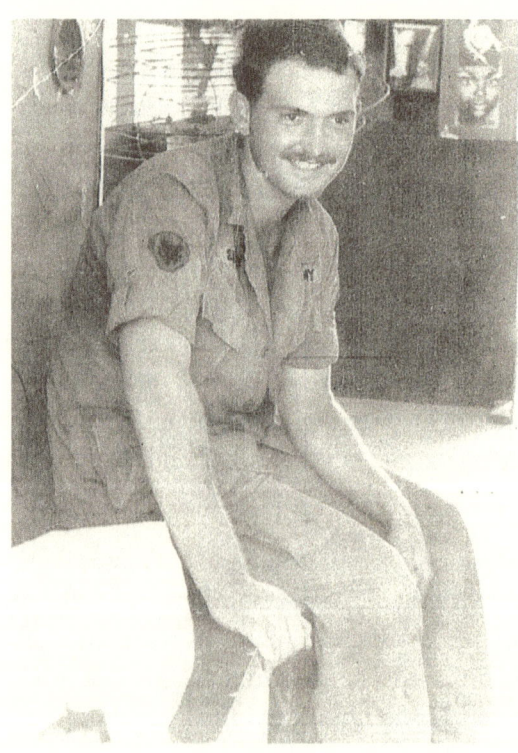

JULY 4, 1969

Just after midnight a young couple was attacked at the Blue Rock Springs Golf Course parking lot in Vallejo. It was Darlene Ferrin and Mike Mageau. Darlene was DOA at the hospital. Mike was treated for multiple gunshot wounds, in critical condition. Mike had been wearing an assortment of clothing consisting of three pairs of trousers, one T-shirt, three sweaters and one-lone sleeved button shirt. These items of clothing were received and placed into evidence. Vallejo is typically extremely hot in the middle of summer, even in the evening. According to the police report, the couple had stopped at the parking lot where they could talk on the way to get something to eat. Darlene was driving her Corvair.

Darlene turned the lights and motor off and had the radio playing. Mike reported that they were there just a very short time, a few minutes, and three cars pulled into the parking lot where they were. They were apparently young kids and they heard some laughing and carrying on and a few firecrackers were set off, then the three vehicles left within a short time. This was a very short space of time, a few minutes. Shortly after this, and about five minutes before the shooting occurred, Mike said a vehicle pulled into the lot, coming from the direction of Springs Road and Vallejo.

The driver turned the lights off on the car and pulled around to the left or east side of their car, approximately six or eight feet away and sat there for a minute. Mike said he asked Darlene if she knew who it was and she stated, "oh never mind." Although he recalled the shape of the car was similar to Darlene's Corvair, he could not see the color as it was very dark out there, but that as far a he could tell, this car had one man in it. The car then drove off and headed in the direction of Vallejo and Springs Road at a fairly fast speed. Approximately five minutes later the vehicle coming from the direction of Vallejo and Springs Road pulled up approximately ten feet behind and to the right side of Darlene's car, which would be the side Mike was sitting. The vehicle's lights were left on and the subject got out and walked toward the car. He had a large high-powered flashlight, the kind you carry with a handle. This subject walked up to the car and Mike stated that both he and Darlene believed that it was a policeman and that he wanted to check their I.D. or something. The subject did not say anything to them, nor did they say anything to him. Michael said he started to reach for his wallet as he felt it was a policeman who wanted to see his I.D.

As he did so, he heard a muffled sound and felt a pain in his back and neck area. Mike heard more muffled sounds that sounded like a gun with a silencer on it as it was not loud. He felt pains in his body, his back, and around his neck. Mike tried to climb over the back seat to get away from the shooter and subject kept shooting him again and again. Finally the subject quit shooting him and apparently turned the gun on Darlene and started shooting her again and again. The subject turned around and casually walked back to his vehicle and got in.

When asked if he could give a description of the man, Mike said he appeared to be short, possibly 5'8 in height, and aged in the late twenties, real heavy set with a beefy build, possibly two hundred pounds or maybe even heavier. He had short curly hair, light brown, almost blonde, and was wearing a short-sleeved shirt, blue in color. There was nothing unusual about his face, other than it appeared to be large. He did not have a mustache, nor was he wearing glasses. Mike could not recall anything unusual except that he had a large face. Mike re-emphasized that he really did not get a good look at subject other than his profile. It was dark out and hard to see the subject.

Mike was questioned as to a possible motive, if he had any argument or trouble, etc. with anyone recently, or if there was any reason at all anyone would want to harm him. He stated he could not recall anything at all, having not had any arguments or anything to give anyone reason to do something like this. Mike said that Darlene did not say anything about any trouble that she had had; they have always been very truthful with each other and confided very closely in each other's problems and he was sure if she had known about someone after her or had a hate for her enough to do something like this, she would have said something about it.

I'm in Vietnam and get a letter from Bob:

July 6, 1969: I arrived at the 101st Airborne Division processing area in Da Nang. I completed P training then was assigned to a small direct support echelon Ordnance Co. located in I Corps. The 101st base camps were located off Highway 1, the coastal route from Saigon to Hanoi. Camp Eagle, located ten kilometers southeast of Hue was division headquarters. The 1st Brigade was located at the nearby Phu Bai Combat Base. The 2nd Brigade was at Landing Zone Sally about ten kilometers northwest of Hue; further up Highway 1 was Camp Evans.

July 10, 1969: I arrived at Camp Eagle a French Vietnamese graveyard we shared with Third Division Marines. Soon I was reunited with the now Chief Warrant Officer Robert Bigley at the 801st Ordnance 101 Airborne Division. I began working TDY at the 801st and maintained another ' Armament Float'. I received a small collection of undocumented weapons [SKS, AK-47's and a few AK-50's with serial numbers ground off from SOG operations is North Vietnam] at the 67th Ordnance 1st Logistical Command from Specialist 5th class Ken Kissling. These weapons were "trading items" at this stage in the war...

SOG: [Special Operations Group and later Studies & Observations Group] Special Forces and Airborne Rangers who carried out black operations and gray propaganda in North Vietnam that included attacking military and civilian installations on the north coast]. I was officially assigned and all my mail was sent to me at the 67th. But one day I got a letter from Bob Hemphill addressed to me at the 801st. I was shocked how could he have known? He wrote, "You been doing your share of killing over there? I've been doing my share over here, been watching some of your relatives. You mail this or I will start killing more of your family."

General Westmoreland's war of attrition taking and giving up hills in the A Shau Valley was taking its toll on morale. As the 101st pulled out of the A Shau shortly after all the bloodshed at Dong Ap Bia and, based on intelligence reports of enemy buildup in the low lands on the minds of some, losing the war in I Corps during the summer of 1969 became a real possibility. Westmoreland was winning his war on paper in an air conditioned trailer, but brave Americans were losing the war in blood on the battlefield. Taking Hill 937 from the 29th Regiment 324th NVA Division had just killed one hundred and wounded over four hundred Screaming Eagles. The base camp was almost deserted, teams cutting locks off foot lockers and packing up personal belonging to ship to families in the world.

Outrage, racial violence, heroin and fragging [assassination of a superior officer with a fragmentation grenade] soon made its way to Camps Eagle and Evans. A staff sergeant whose name I don't recall was riding on the front of an M88 (tank recovery vehicle) slipped and was crushed to death under the huge track.The sergeant wasn't a close friend but his death shocked everyone. A buddy from South Pasadena and I wanted to get away even if only in our heads, so we dropped some orange acid sent to me by a friend from Sunol. The catalyst for the experience was tension among heads, draftees and lifers, along with the uncertainty of what was going to come out of it. The effects of battlefield consciousness on psychedelics were frightful. We tripped on an AH-1 G Cobra gunships automatic cannon and 6-barrel mini-gun firing from overhead toward an NVA .51 caliber machine gun firing from the mountains near Fire Support Base Panther 11. Red (USA) - white (NVA) tracers collide then ricochet and fracture the night.

As the fog rolled in we put smudge pots out behind the bunkers. We started eating stuff and smoking weed to try to come down from the acid - the Dragon was on the way. I didn't touch the letter for days; mind blown and troubled with the realization that you can run but you can never hide... Hemphill's gang stalking had just as much control over me here as it did when I was still in the East Bay. I mailed the letter from Camp Eagle APO SF 96383.

July 31, 1969: Shortly after Darlene's murder the San Francisco Chronicle, the San Francisco Examiner and the Vallejo Times Herald received letters from her killer. Zodiac was introduced in part of a three-page letter sent to the Vallejo Times Herald.

Zodiacs Cryptograms:

August 1969 the San Francisco Chronicle received a cryptogram from Darlene's killer. (Later February 1986 Bob would tell me that my name is mentioned). I found my name in one of the three-part portion that was sent to the SF Chronicle then decoded by the Harden's.

Line #1: DAVE   Line #2 and 6: SILVEY

Line #8: In the last line, is the name Darlene knew Bob by; the name on CIA ID Bob used at Fort Lewis Visitors center and the name he used to recruit mercenaries at Hanau West Germany. Bob HEMPHILL

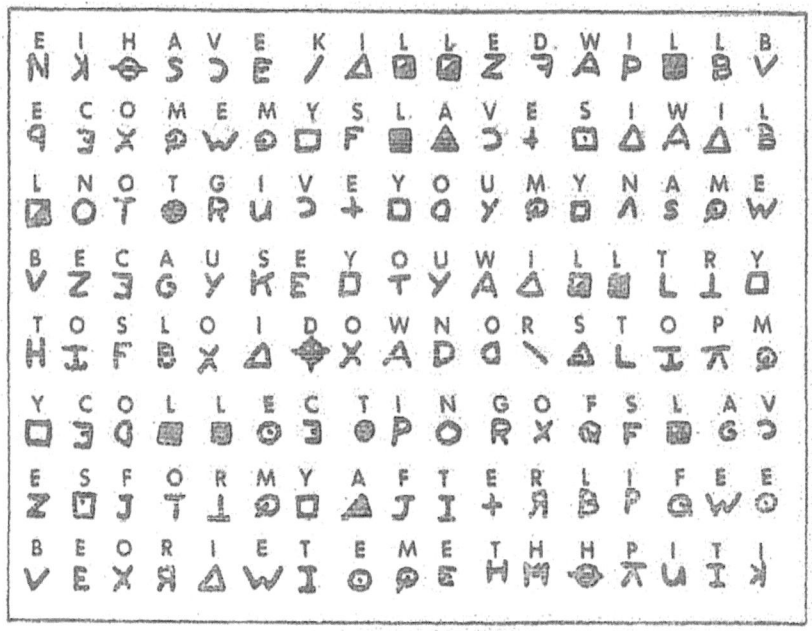

September 27, 1969: Bryan Hartnell and Cecelia Shepard both college students picnicking at Lake Berryessa in Napa County when a tall man wearing a hooded costume ties them up with rope and stabs them with a foot long knife. Shepard dies, Hartnell survives.

Tom Pains wife Kathy Anderson's [her maiden name] bother Mike Hayner would tell me later in 1987 that he went camping with his brother in law Tom Pain and Bob Hemphill at Lake Berryessa the day of the attack in 1969. Bob Hemphill brought a motorcycle that he and Tom Pain left on, leaving Mike Hayner alone at the Camp site. He drove Bob Hemphill's white Chevy back to Sunol himself, Mike was fifteen years old at the time. He was the one that went into the store at Lake Berryessa asking for direction. Mike also said there was a small white door wrapped in a blanket in the trunk of the Chevy, when he got home it was gone.

At this point in the war I lost two friends to drugs, Enrich Ceresco a hard core Mexican dude from Odessa Texas went AWOL in Hue just before he was to return home. He had a heavy addiction to herion. Another friend, a tough paratrooper named Marino from Tucson Arizona got busted for drugs, court marshaled and sent to Leavenworth Prison.

October 11, 1969: At 3898 Washington Street in San Francisco three teenagers watched from the second floor windows approximately fifty feet away as the assailant struggled with the cab driver after shooting him in the head. Unlike some of the others, Paul Stine could possibly be a confirmed Zodiac victim who was not a hypnotic subject. The assailant left the scene covered in the cab driver's blood. Two patrolmen arrived and questioned a man some blocks away from the scene but did not detain him. The police composite poster generated later by eyewitness accounts was incredibly accurate on both men. Most believe it to be an amended composite of one man 'Zodiac'.

The witness's and patrolman did an excellent job on their descriptions, Tom Pain on the left side and Bob Hemphill on the right.

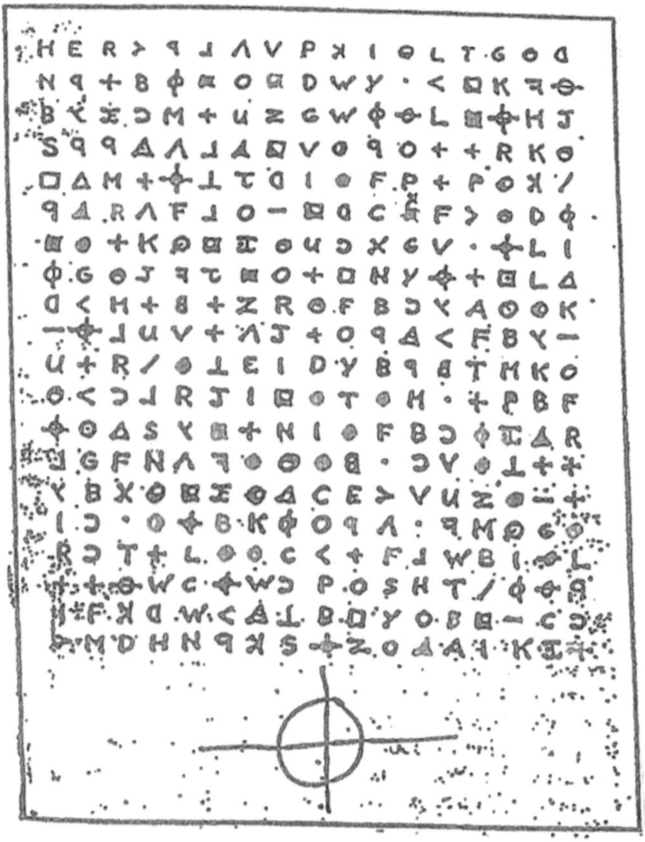

incredibly accurate on both men. Most believe it to be an amended composite of one man 'Zodiac'.

WANTED

SAN FRANCISCO POLICE DEPARTMENT

| NO. 90-69 | WANTED FOR MURDER | OCTOBER 18, 1969 |

ORIGINAL DRAWING   AMENDED DRAWING

Supplementing our Bulletin 87-69 of October 13, 1969. Additional information has developed the above amended drawing of murder suspect known as "ZODIAC".

WMA, 35-45 Years, approximately 5'8", Heavy Build, Short Brown Hair, possibly with Red Tint, Wears Glasses. Armed with 9 MM Automatic.

Available for comparison: Slugs, Casings, Latents, Handwriting.

ANY INFORMATION:
Inspectors Armstrong & Toschi
Homicide Detail
CASE NO. 696314

THOMAS J. CAHILL
CHIEF OF POLICE

October 13, 1969: The northern monsoon season begins and life is much tougher. Even when the rains let up dense fog moves in. Back in the world the Chronicle receives a letter containing a bloody swatch of Stine's shirt and a threat to shoot children on a school bus.

November 8, 1969: San Francisco Police Inspector Dave Toschi received the Zodiac's 340-symbol cipher imbedded with an RFK assassination clue. A day later I was ordered to MACV headquarters in Hue to inspect a weapon used in an apparent suicide [a last-bullet-for-yourself type of thing]. GI's were carrying a single suicide bullet in the camo band of their helmets for fear of torture; many felt that we were about to lose the war. I met the 1st lieutenant (CID) requesting the inspection. I was surprised to see that it was an M-14 rifle without a scope. This was not Army general issue and was kind of rare at this point in the war. During the inspection I noticed disappointment on the Lieutenant's face. I informed him that I was checking for malfunction or signs of cook-off that could have made it discharge. He stated, "No you're not holding it the way I need you to. Fact is I need your prints to compare against latent prints back in the world." I figured that it had to do with the letter or M-14's that I procured for Bob in Germany and I agreed to let him roll my prints on a print card.

November 10, 1969: The Chronicle receives another letter from the Zodiac containing detailed plans for a death machine to blow up a school bus.

Visit at Camp Eagle from Fed investigator and same fellow from Germany:

Late 1969: A Federal investigator who was with the same individual that I had met in the Green Arrow Hotel Casino at Garmisch contacted me and wanted to talk. They requested that I be unarmed and meet them at the 3rd Marine Division side of Camp Eagle. The one doing all the talking was WMA, had a stocky powerful build aged in his forties and dressed in Marine fatigues. He wanted me to read from the "Official Government Report on Assassination of Robert F. Kennedy". The portion that I read described a .22 Cal. Revolver with 'AL SILVEY' (the name of my father) engraved on the receiver. It was reportedly found on the floor in the pantry near where the assassination took place at the Ambassador Hotel. I told them everything that I have said here about what I know of the assassination. He knew about the incident involving the M14's in West Germany and he asked a few questions concerning the attempted assassination of Papa Doc. The rifles were match quality and belonged to an elite army rifle team he was puzzled. He stated, "You're not a member of Al Hilal I am and I know you're not." I replied that I have never said I was a member. The investigator then asked, "What do you know about the kids who were shot in Vallejo. It was a hit what do you know about silencers?" This was the first time I heard about Darlene's murder, I didn't know what to say. He then asked if I was stoned and he wanted to know how potent the weed in Vietnam was. I laughed and made a comment without warning he put me in a chokehold and yelled, "Bob Kennedy was my friend." They left me on the bunker gasping for breath.

March 22, 1970: Kathleen Johns, 22 and her newborn daughter are traveling on Highway 132 west of Modesto when a man in a car offers to help them tighten the nuts on a loose rim, then disables the vehicle and gives them a ride under the guise of driving them to a service station. The man then drives them around for several hours without stopping. Johns escapes by jumping out the door with her infant and later identifies her kidnapper as the man depicted in a 1969 SFPD Wanted Poster for the Zodiac.

April 28, 1970 I received notification concerning my R&R plans to meet my girlfriend Sandy Anderson in Waikiki; we would meet at the Maluhia Service Club at Fort De Russy. Just days before my R&R with Sandy I am wounded by a booby trapped weapon and shipped home.

May 5, 1970: The monsoon rains began to clear up and the NVA moved into the lowlands. While working with the 801st inspecting captured weapons that probably traveled from the Warehouse area (nicknamed because of the huge weapon caches found there) in the mountains northeast of the A Shau Valley, down NVA supply routes ending up in an ambush on the Perfume River. While clearing the captured weapons I was blown up by a booby trapped Rocket Propelled Grenade (RPG), possibly as a result of top secret CIA Operation code named 'Eldest Son', or even worse a direct attempt to dispose of me.

I survived and was at the 85th EVAC in Da Nang on a stretcher in the hallway waiting to board a medical transport plane when the Marine investigator who jumped me at Camp Eagle approached, the last person I spoke to in Vietnam! He said, "When you can disappear, do something with your life." I was then MEDEVAC to Letterman General Hospital in San Francisco via Osaka, Japan and Travis Air Base.

Bob visits me at Letterman Hospital:

My father was the first person to visit after I arrived at Letterman Hospital and as we talked I noticed Hemphill standing in the doorway. Bob came in behind my father, opened his P-coat to show me a blue steel semi-automatic, it looked like a Browning High Power 9 mm. He took off his safety glasses and was glaring at me as my father left; he then came closer to the bed. As I tried to get out of bed I hit him with an IV pole, the bottle broke and the needle pulled out of my arm. He said, "I'm living a couple blocks away, I'll see you later fuck head."

The next day two nurses came into my room and accused me of being an imposter. One of them was very upset and insisted that I was not David Silvey. I didn't know either of them and offered to help clear it up any way they wanted but they both left in tears. I subsequently learned that Tom Pain was dating a nurse in San Francisco and was using my ID.

May 31, 1970: Bob Postel visited me at Letterman with bad news:

Bob Ussery, my good friend from boyhood on had just drowned at a small private pond in Sunol. The pond was isolated, located behind a locked gate and hidden from sight. Bob had returned from Vietnam and was recently discharged from the army in excellent shape. He was a strong swimmer who didn't swim alone no one believes it was an accident. A witness, Don Holderfield reported, "Yes, I was there with Bob and Tony. That is something everyone else knows too. Tony could not swim and I am not a strong swimmer. I did go out and try to get him. We all thought he was joking around. No, we had not been drinking. It just happened. I don't know why. All I know is it did. It's not something I like to remember. If you have any other questions you can ask his brother, or any member of his family. There were people there neither of us Knew on the other side of the pond."

San Francisco Water Company pond [below].

July 10, 1970: Released from Letterman General Hospital and I was considering the investigator's advice to disappear. Sandy picked me up at the Hospital and she drove to my parent's new home on Bethel Island. The first words out of my mothers' mouth when we got there, "To bad you didn't get killed over there, we could have been proud of you". I laughed, Sandy went ballistic, and my father took her for a boat ride to calm things down. When they got back she was still upset so we left.

July 26, 1970: The Chronicle receives another letter from the Zodiac in which he makes an unsubstantiated claim of killing 13 people.

August 1970 Partying up Kilkare Canyon I got into a wreck and was arrested for being AWOL from the ARMY. I ended up at the infamous Presidio Stockade, my body painted with psychedelic body paint. That was enough for an ass whipping, but they in the process dislocated my shoulder by spraying me with a high pressure fire hose while handcuffed... I was in the emergency room at Letterman Hospital and complained about my treatment at the hands of MP's at the stockade to the doctor's.

The next morning I was transferred to Fort Ord Special Processing Detachment from the Presidio Stockade. I could have visitors at SPD, Sandy and friends from Sunol came to see me.

SILVEY, DAVID M   S 410

SSDC MRN   SOCIAL SECURITY NO.

3. DATE EAD OR ENLISTED 29 FEB 68   4. TERM OF ENL. (Months) 36   8. NO. OF TAX EXEMPTIONS CZ

10. ORGANIZATION AND ADDRESS (Include ZIP Code)

11. REMARKS
WIA   5May 70
NOT ENT CMAE CAS RVN

MILITARY PAY VOUCHER

6. PAY PERIOD: 1-30 JUN 70   8. TAXABLE INCOME CZ

290.10

290 10

18 75

SOLT   46   2 00
SH   23   1 20

TOTAL ENTITLEMENTS 951 355 23
TOTAL COLLECTIONS 902 35 87
AMOUNT DUE 903 319 36
AMOUNT PAID 26 319 36
AMOUNT UNPAID CARRIED FORWARD 27

FICA TAX WITHHELD 29 13 93
INCOME TAX WITHHELD 21 0
TOTAL COLLECTIONS 902 35 87

FOR H.D. FLYNN, CPT FC   3 JUN 70

62 AMOUNT SHOWN AS PAID ACKNOWLEDGED

433044

DA FORM 1 OCT 63 2139

Form Approved by Comptroller General, U.S., 10 Jul 1956

Payee 4

August 12, 1970 I got a visit from Bob Hemphill:

He asked me if I wanted out, I said I did. "I'll take care of it; you call somebody to get back to Sunol". I asked what happen with Bob Ussery. He didn't answer, just walked away. I walked over to the payphone to make the call; they would pick me up in the morning around 11:00 am. Two MP's came over and started giving me and another guy trouble for being outside and out of uniform; I had no fatigues or hat. They locked me into a steal wire in-processing cage inside the MP office barracks near the mess hall. Because of my shoulder, they made the other guy carry mattresses up stairs and clean the restrooms. I fell asleep on the narrow wooden bench.

Later that evening, I woke up to the sounds of a crowd yelling and three MP's unlocked the cage and ran out of the building. When I came out of the barracks I could see that it was on fire and the mess hall next door was also on fire. When the fire department came the rioters took the truck over and went through several hundred feet of cyclone fence and drove off to Monterey.

MP's armed with shotguns surrounded the rest of us who didn't take the excursion ride to Monterey on the fire truck. This lasted until daybreak; we slept on the dirt... I was separated from the group because I was still in civilian clothes. I was given an opportunity to shower and was given fatigues to wear.

 I was brought back to the group and we were marched to another mess hall a few blocks away. I spoke to the guy who got into trouble as I did for not being in uniform. He told me that they talked to my buddy through the fence and he said that he called the LA Times and the San Francisco Chronicle to report the riot.

I was interviewed and questioned about what I knew and saw last night. On the way back to the detachment a block or so away I waited by the dumpsters for my ride home.

Within a few minutes they showed and we went to the beach to relax. After a few beers I thought it would be better for me to go back. As we turned off the freeway at the Fort Ord exit we could see MP's searching cars coming in and going out. We got back on the freeway.

Monterey Peninsula Herald: August 13, 1970: Two wooden mess halls at the Special Processing Detachment at Fort Ord were gutted by fire last night. Today, men assigned to the unit threatened to burn more buildings tonight. "We used matches last night, "a young soldier told Herald reporter this morning. "Tonight we'll use gasoline. We've got a five gallon can."

Commenting on the threat of arson activity tonight, a Fort Ord spokesman said later: "Needless to say, the place will be closely watched." Damage to the mess halls were estimated to be five to ten thousand dollars.

The Special Processing Detachments, a unit of limited confinement for men who may be waiting trial or transfer to a Stockade or whose administrative papers may have been lost. Many of the men also are AWOL violators being detained in what is called 'post confinement' a form of detention much less restrictive than a stockade.

A non-barbed cyclone fence surrounds the barracks buildings and other structures of the detachment. Men assigned to the unit can receive passes to move about elsewhere on the post and in somewhat rare circumstances, may even receive passes to leave the post.

The mess hall fires broke out one after the other, about 9 o'clock – shortly after a relatively minor disturbance possibly related to alleged harassment assigned to the detachment by military police. Army sources said that the two buildings "went up" so quickly that they believed flammable liquids had been used.

The Army said, "The minor disturbance involved some twenty-five to thirty men of the approximately three hundred men assigned to the detachment." A spokesman said, "The men began shouting but it was not clear what they were shouting about. After a period of time, they quieted down by themselves. Then about ten minutes later, one of the mess halls went up in flames and then the other."

The Army declared this morning that it had no motives and no suspects. An investigation was launched by the Provost Marshal's office and by a special administrative team appointed by Maj. Gen. Philip B. Davidson, commanding general.

While the Army said it had no motives, a number of the detachment's men readily told a Herald reporter that the fires had been set because they were angered at the MP's. Surrounded by his buddies, one man pressed against the fence to say in effect that he was a central figure in the action.

He said that some MP's came inside the fence last night and "busted him" for not wearing a hat. He said the MP's grabbed him and a friend and took them off to an MP office. There, he said some superiors of the MP' told the MP's that if these men (the two soldiers) gave them any more trouble they were free to do whatever they wanted with them... The two soldiers were then returned to the detachment area.

Other soldiers who were clustered about the reporter shouted that the MP's had no right to come inside the compound. Apparently feeling that they had a good listener, the fatigue clad soldiers went on to invite the reporter to come back tonight for the "SPD" luau."

Also in late 1970: Tom Pain would brag of his achievements in fragments here, the cab driver he killed:

Later I saw Tom in Sunol, I asked what happen to Bob Ussery? He started bragging that he was using my name to date a nurse in San Francisco. He further told me about killing a cab driver, then leaving the City covered in his blood. Bob was there but not close enough to be seen and he had no blood on him. Tom burned his shirt, pants and underwear at his mother's house on Foothill Road then claims he walked up the hill to his home and had sex with his wife Kathy.

THE ORDER

July 8, 1974: In the last verified Zodiac letter to the Chronicle, the Zodiac complains about columnist Count Marco, who he says always, needs to feel superior to everyone.

October 29, 1974:

I saw Dave Mullins in Sunol and he spoke of Bob planning something to resolve everything so we can get on with our lives. He wants us to come to a meeting with Tony Pine and other people from Sunol. We met Bob in Sunol and he drove us in his white Chevy to the Salinas River where it flows into the ocean at Moss Landing.

We had to be there at midnight of course, I was surprised to see Dr. Bryan dressed up in a black KKK looking gown with the pointed hood, the movie cameras and lighting was all in place and generators were running. There was an armed triple roving perimeter. This is going to sound stupid but just like in the movies as it got closer to midnight dark clouds started to form just above us. A God fearing – Devil worshiping ceremony was about to bring Al Hilal and Four P into The Order.+

There was a crowd of around twenty five to thirty people dressed in costumes, a masquerade on the other side of the river with the flags and banners. Tony Pine was there with a few other people from Sunol .A huge star who used to live in Sunol was also standing on our side of the river. Bob introduced me to a young guy named Robbie Mathews. Dr. Bryan did his thing spinning around yelling stuff I couldn't hear or even begin to understand. Then he took of the hood and started to talk to us directly. "Al Hilal and FOUR P are moving forward as The Order"

Bob started talking, "Over the next ten years the group will continue to operate like Al Hilal and FOUR P but work as a mercenary venture raising money.. Over the next ten years we will continue to assassinate tyrants". Bob came over to me and said, "Lets take a walk." We walked up the Salinas River and we met Tom Pain and two other guys. Bob then introduced Jim Sanders to me and said we would be working together at Brinks; "You guys will be on the inside." Then Bob told Jim that I was the Zodiac, I laughed, and Jim said that he's heard of me. We all laughed!

Bob and Tom got behind these guys with government model 45's pointed at their heads and said, "What do you think, can they be trusted? Give us the word and their dead". I told Jim, "I'll see you in ten years at Brink's!" I didn't know what to make of this, being AWOL from the Army Special Processing Detachment - Brink's is going to hire me? Nothing got resolved and I decided to blow this whole thing off. Over the years it was easy to forget.

December 5, 1975: I received clemency and was discharged from the U.S. Armed Forces under Presidential Proclamation 4313. I tried hard to forget these ever-haunting and emotional draining events. I married my girlfriend and raised our three children, worked and paid taxes. I attended night classes in a veterans program at San Jose State University. Joint Hearings before the Select Committee on Intelligence and the Subcommittee on Health and Scientific Research of the U.S. SENATE were well under way in their investigation into Project MK-ULTRA, the CIA's program of research in behavioral modification.

WILLIAM TURNER:

Our quest for Sirhans' programmer had been no more successful than the search for Amelia Earhart until Dr. Herbert Spiegel gave us a lead. Anything mentioned in presence of a subject under hypnosis automatically etched into his mind, especially if it comes from the hypnotist.

And it might flow out at any time. This brought us back to the notebooks containing Sirhan's automatic writing. Could he have scrawled something during a trance regression that the hypnotist had mentioned while programming him?

There was a passage that stood out because it was unlike the others, having nothing to do with horses, politics, money or past acquaintances. It read god help me please help me. Salvo Di Salvo Di Salvo.

The reference apparently was to Albert Di Salvo, the notorious Boston Strangler. That case had been cracked by the use of hypnotism and the hypnotist was Dr. William J. Bryan Jr., of Los Angeles.

Bryan billed himself as probably the leading expert in the world on the use of hypnosis in criminal law and often boasted about being called into baffling cases by law enforcement agencies, including the LAPD. The Boston Strangler case was his tour de force and he was incessantly mentioning it.

An imposing man with a wrestler's girth, Bryan claimed he was once drummer with the Tommy Dorsey band and a commercial airplane pilot. During the Korean War he had put his hypnotic skills to use as in his words, chief of all medical survival training for the United States Air Force, which meant the brainwashing section.

After the war he reportedly became a CIA consultant in the Agency's experimentation with mind control and behavior modification. Refused membership in all traditional medical societies, Bryan set up a medical and hypnotherapy practice on Sunset Strip in Hollywood, which he named the American Institute of Hypnosis.

He used it as an aegis for wide-ranging symposiums on such topics as 'Successful Treatments of Sexual Disorders'. "I enjoy variety and I like to get to know people on a deep emotional level, One way of getting to know people is through intercourse" he once told a magazine interviewer.

In 1969, the California Board of Medical Examiners found him guilty of unprofessional conduct for sexually molesting four women patients who submitted under hypnosis. Bryan was given five years probation on the condition that he has an adult woman present whenever treating female patients.

Despite his advocacy of sexual freedom, Dr. Bryan was a Bible quoting fundamentalist who belonged to a fire and brimstone sect called the Old Roman Catholic Church.

Curiously, David W Ferrie, a prime suspect in New Orleans District Attorney Jim Garrisons 1967 probe into the John Kennedy assassination, also belonged to this small sect. Ferrie was found dead on February 22, 1967, shortly after being interrogated. Bryan claimed to be a descendant of the fiery orator William Jennings Bryan who opposed the teaching of evolution in the celebrated Scopes 'monkey trial' and he was frequently a guest preacher at several fundamentalist churches in Southern California."

Only hours after the RFK shooting and before Sirhan had been identified, Dr. Bryan appeared on the Los Angeles radio talk show program of Ray Briem (KABC) and off handedly commented that "the suspect probably acted under post hypnotic suggestion".

Spring 1977: Dr. William J. Bryan was found dead in a Las Vegas motel room: The cause of death was publicly declared natural causes.

August 3, 1977: Joint Hearings before the Select Committee on Intelligence and the Subcommittee on Health and Scientific Research of the U.S.SENATE concluded their investigation into Project MK-ULTRA, the CIA's program of research in behavioral modification.

The Subcommittee on Health and Scientific Research of the U.S. Senate Chairman Senator Edward Kennedy:

Some two years ago, the Senate Health Subcommittee heard chilling testimony about the human experimentation activities of the Central Intelligence Agency. The Deputy Director of the CIA revealed that over thirty universities and institutions were involved in an extensive testing and experimentation program which included covert drug tests on unwitting citizens at all social levels, high and low, native American and foreign. Unwitting subjects in social situations. At least one death that of Dr. Olson resulted from these activities.

The agency itself acknowledged that these tests made little scientific sense. The agents doing the monitoring were not qualified scientific observers.

The test subjects were seldom accessible beyond the first hours of the test. In a number of instances, these test subjects became ill for hours or days, and effective following was impossible. Other experiments were equally offensive. For example, heroin addicts were enticed into participating in LSD experiments in order to get a reward heroin.

Perhaps most disturbing of all was the fact that the extent of experimentation on human subjects was unknown. The records of all these activities were destroyed in January 1973, at the instruction of then CIA Director Helms. In spite of persistent inquiries by both the Health Subcommittee and the Intelligence Committee, no additional records or information were forthcoming. And no single individual could be found who remembered the details, nor the Director of the CIA, who ordered the documents destroyed, not the official responsible for the program, nor any of his associates.

We believed that the record, incomplete as it was, was as complete as it was going to be. Then one individual; through a Freedom of Information request, accomplished what two U.S. Senate committees could not. He spurred the agency into finding additional records pertaining to the CIA's program of experimentation with human subjects. These new records were discovered by the Agency in March. Their existence was not made known to the Congress until July. The records reveal a far more extensive series of experiments than had previously been thought. Eighty-six universities were involved. New instances of unethical behavior were revealed.

The intelligence community of this Nation, which requires a shroud of secrecy in order to operate, has a very sacred trust from the American people. The CIA's program of human experimentation of the fifties and sixties violated that trust. It is violated each time a responsible officer refuses to recollect the details of the program. The best safeguard against abuses in the future is a complete public accounting of the abuses of the past.

During the fall of 1980, I went to North Livermore Avenue, the safe house where I had the encounter with Bryan, Sirhan and Darlene just before RFK's assassination. I went out of curiosity and found that the old church was now a pile of rubble, the eucalyptus trees had burn marks, and it looked like what remained was bulldozed. The house looked abandoned I noticed some windows on the second floor were still boarded up and the black Cadillac was there it was creepy, so I took some pictures then left right away.

During the summer 1981 I applied to a job advertisement in the Oakland Tribune for Brink's Inc:

I spoke to Randy Johnson, the area manager on the phone; he encouraged me to meet him at the Hilton Hotel in Fremont. When I got into the lobby I saw a guy looking for somebody and introduced myself, his name was Jim Sanders, he said that he was here to meet Randy Johnson from Brink's.

"If you remember Jim Sanders from the meeting on Salinas River this is going to be unbelievable," but neither one of us remembered anything. Although Jim did say "you look familiar." At the time I had no memory of our meeting in 1974.

We both interviewed and got hired by Brink's and became partners for three years.

Until I became messenger of the shuttle run that started from San Francisco and met with south bay runs in Milpitas to switch loads. At the end of the day picked up loads from south bay runs and shuttled back to San Francisco. While Jim and I were still on the same run he told me about his father leaving him at a chicken farm in Fremont during the late 50's, Jim said "They killed people there!" The hair on my neck stood up as I wondered. In my mind if Jim was the kid my mother pulled out of the car at Ike Feldman's chicken ranch... I didn't know what to say and said nothing; the connection was very weird and painful. It all escalated when Jim accused me of being the Zodiac Killer.

July 19, 1984: The Order robs Brink's Ukiah run:

My driver Cary Stevens told me when I got back into the truck that Lisa was on the radio calling for help," The Ukiah run got hit. Shots fired!"

On Lisa's return to work Brink's paid me to follow her for a couple of runs to make sure she was ok. Lisa King, the pretty redhead was Ron King's wife.

║║║BRINKS

Brink's Armored Car, Inc.
Thorndal Circle
P.O. Box 1225
Darien, Connecticut 06820-0473
203-655-8781
Cable Address: BRINKSINC
Telex: 965-852

TEMPORARY IDENTIFICATION NOTICE

A Subsidiary of Brink's, Incorporated

BRINK'S
San Jose, California Branch

August 8, 1984

Facsimile signatures, for the purpose of identification, of all employees at the branch indicated above who are presently authorized to endorse and cash checks made payable to this corporation or its order and to call for shipments and to receipt therefor are as shown on this notice:-

In case there is any question as to the authority of the person presenting himself as a Brink's representative, please phone our office at 415 431-8640 to verify the status of the individual.

R. T. Johnson   C. Stevens

M. Grealis   J. L. Cygan

J. Zerbe   K. Franklin

L. King

D. Davis

J. Sanders

D. Silvey

Wm. Walker

You are cautioned to compare actual signatures of all persons who may represent themselves to have such authority as is referred to herein with the facsimile signatures.

This notice is effective until further notice is given and supersedes all prior notices.

BRINK'S ARMORED CAR, INC.

68

R. T. Johnson, District Manager S.F.

Oakland Tribune article by Steve Robtalle:

FBI agents arrested two reputed members of a white supremacist group, one Hayward man, Wednesday morning in connection with a conspiracy to rob the main vault at the San Francisco headquarters of Brink's Inc.

FBI officials said the arrests are part of an ongoing investigation of a Neo-Nazi group called "The Order" believed to be responsible for the $3.6 million robbery last July of a Brink's armored car in Ukiah.

Ronald Allen King (45) of 221 Sunset Blvd in Hayward, a Brink's operations manager employed by the company for 18 years, was arrested at his home about 9 a.m. by agents from the FBI's San Francisco Office, said special agent Robert Deklinski.

Charles E. Ostrout, (51), a Brink's money room supervisor since 1981, was arrested about the same time at his home in Lookout, a town in southern Modoc County, by agents from the FBI's Sacramento office, Deklinski said.

The two men, both on disability leave from Brink's were arrested on suspicion of conspiracy to rob the company's main cash vault, and Ostrout also was arrested on suspicion of helping to plan and execute the Ukiah armored car robbery, Deklinski said.

The two men, the first Brink's employees to be arrested in connection with the Ukiah holdup, reportedly provided detailed information on group members that aided in the planning of that robbery, according to an affidavit filed in U.S. District court in San Francisco by Special agent Patrick Webb.

But only Ostrout will be charged with the Ukiah robbery because there is not enough evidence to prosecute King in the case, said Assistant U.S. Attorney Peter Robinson. Brink's issued a statement Wednesday that said the company has cooperated with the FBI and support their efforts resolving the situation.

King bearded, heavyset man appeared before U.S. Magistrate F. Steele Langford in San Francisco Wednesday afternoon and was appointed a public defender. He is being held without bail pending a Monday bail hearing. Ostrout was scheduled to appear today before a federal magistrate in Sacramento, Robinson said.

Deklinski would not say when group members planned to rob the cash vault or how they planned to pull off the heist at Brink's 12th Street headquarters. The FBI affidavit stated that an informant who participated in the Ukiah robbery said King provided group members with information about the San Francisco cash vault, including security procedures, floor plans and alarm systems.

The informant also said Ostrout allegedly provided group members with information about the route to be traveled by the Ukiah armored van, the amount of money carried on that particular run and the composition of the crew, according to the FBI affidavit.

The FBI located King and Ostrout through telephone records of a call made to San Lorenzo apartment the two men shared until last October, according to the FBI affidavit. The call was made two days before the Ukiah robbery from a booth outside a Santa Rosa motel where the Ukiah robbery suspects were believed to be staying.

The two men shared the apartment during the week and Ostrout would commute to Lookout on his off days, the FBI said, King moved to Hayward in October. The Order affiliated with an Idaho-based white supremacist group called the Aryan Nation; planned to finance a program of assassination and guerrilla movements through a series of robberies, according to the FBI.

The FBI said twelve group members carried out the July 19, 1984, Ukiah robbery, which was led by reputed group leader Robert Mathews. Mathews suspected of the November 1984 shooting an FBI agent in Portland Ore. died in a shootout and fire with FBI agents Dec. 8 in a cottage on Whidbey Island, Wash.

Within the past month, the FBI has arrested four others Ukiah robbery suspects in Washington, Oregon and Montana, and all four eventually will be brought to San Francisco to stand trail, Deklinski said.

The Ukiah robbery informant said King and Ostrout formally inducted into the Order last August in San Francisco, the FBI affidavit said.

The group used a voice stress analyzer to try to determine if prospective members were police informants, according to the affidavit.

Next thing I knew I was in the lobby of the FBI office in the Federal in San Francisco. My self, my girl friend Michael Bauer and two Philippine National Brinks SF vault men waiting to be interviewed. I was interviewed by Special agent in charge Tinbinsel for several hours.

CHRONICLE ARTICLE:

Prosecutors' Story of Brink Heist Feb. 13, 1985:

"Neo-Nazi gang members took more than a year to plan last summer's three point six million Brinks armor car robbery in Ukiah and discuss stealing thirty million more in a second Brinks hold up, federal prosecutors said yesterday.

The plot unraveled, however, when one of the thieves left his gun behind during the carefully planned robbery, and FBI agents used it to track down the rest of the group.

Assistant US attorney Robert D Ward discussed some of the details of the group's plans in federal court yesterday doing a detention hearing for two suspects in the robbery, Ronald Allen King (45) and Charles E Ostrout, (51).

King, a Brinks employee for eighteen years, was Operation Manager of the San Francisco office until he went on disability leave last fall, Ostrout, who also is on leave managed the counting room at Brinks.

King, Ostrout and Bruce Carroll Pierce, a fugitive, were indicted last week my federal grand jury that charged them with conspiring to steal a vast sum of money from the persons in presence of employees of Brinks Armor car company.

In addition Ostrout was charged with helping to plan the Ukiah robbery by providing diagrams of the armor cars routes to the thieves, and by advising them how and when to rob the vehicle.

Both men have pleaded not guilty to the charges and are being held without bail at and undisclosed location.

During yesterday's hearing, Ward told us magistrate Steele Lanford that King and Ostrout were members of the "Bruderschweigen" or Brotherhood of Silence. A right wing group that has declared war, in writing, on Jews, the government and minority group members.

Ward said, the members of the organization, which is also known as the Brotherhood, the white American Bastion and the Order, wanted a white man's revolution and they were willing to use murder and robbery to get it.Ward said informants have told federal agents that Ostrout discussed the armor car heist with the founder of the Brotherhood, Robert J Matthews, on several occasions, including a 1963 meeting at Matthews's home in Metaline Falls, Idaho.

Early in the planning, Ostrout suggested a variety of locations for the armor car holdup, including cash transfer points in Milpitas, San Jose and Oakland, Ward said.

Informants said he personally selected the Ukiah location where the robbery ultimately took place and was paid 30,000 dollars from the loot for helping organize the heist, according to Ward.

He added that gang members had also made preliminary plans to rob either the central Brinks vault in San Francisco, or to steal as much as thirty million during cash transfer from Hawaii to the mainland. The thirty million dollar robbery he said, would have taken place when the money was shifted from an airplane to an armor car at San Francisco airport. Both would have been involved in the assault with automatic weapons he said.

In addition to the Ukiah robbery, the Brotherhood participated in a number of banks and armor car heists in Seattle, Ward said. He also linked the bombing at a Synagogue in Boise, ID, although he said he did not know the details.

The attorneys for King and Ostrout asked during the hearing that both men be release on bail because they are long time residents of Northern California with stable work record and are unlikely to flee to avoid prosecution.

Lanford made no decision on the request for bail.

February 1986: I moved into 12245 Foothill Road in Sunol just down the street from where Tom was living with his brother Gerald. Shortly after returning from work, I heard a diesel truck pull up in front of my house. I looked outside to see Bob with a heavy down-type jacket and hands in his pockets. I put my work gun on and answered the door. Bob was shocked to see that I was armed and he tried to walk away. I asked what he wanted, he turned and I put my hand on the butt of my gun and asked him to take his hands out of his pockets he complied. Bob then stated "I've done my share; you know that I'm not going to take any blame for his (Tom's) shit. I have a codebook and some other stuff (Grimoire) that I want you to have. ..... Your name is mentioned in some of the letters, you keep the Grimoire I'll be right back." He then walked back to his truck, took off and did not return

April 30, 1987, I thumbed through Robert Greysmith's Zodiac book while on jury duty:

The 1969 SFPD Wanted Poster for the cab driver's murder caught my eye right away. There was Bob Hemphill on the right side and Tom Pain on the left.

The most chilling part of Greysmith's book was the chapter on Joseph DeLouise, the Chicago psychic. Mental pictures of what Zodiac looked like had been flooding the psychic's mind for almost a month, constantly merging and changing. The image that remained clearest to DeLuoise was that of a man about twenty-eight years old, approximately five foot eight inches tall and weighed between one hundred and thirty five to forty five pounds, with a slightly undernourished look.

"The killer had silky, darkish brown hair that he normally wore in a pompadour, but as disguise combed forward. I don't think Zodiac wears glasses," said Delouise. "He's too vain to wear them even if he needed them. He uses them only as a disguise." This is an incredibly accurate personal description of Bob Hemphill.

The Chicago seer felt that Zodiac used drugs that had damaged his brain and given him a persecution complex, drugs that kept him high, although in the case of the Lake Berryessa murder he was taking some kind of depressant. DeLouise said vibrations he had received, told him that Zodiac had resorted to speed and goof balls, which he took before his murders (LSD, reds and cross tops).

"This man is transmitting," said the psychic. "Only people who deal in this type of extrasensory perception know each other. I hope I can prove to him in some way that I want to help him." DeLouise planned to meet with Chicago police to help develop some sort of composite drawing of his vision.

The seer felt that the killer might be a Scorpio or Aquarian because of the figures '11-2 and 2-11' which he kept receiving, standing for February 11 or November 2 (211 is the only posted address near the front of Bob's house, his address is actually 187 Kilkare 187 is the P.C. Code for murder).

Next, DeLouise visited with Napa law enforcement officials, who went over the details of the Lake Berryessa slaying. DeLouise got new feelings about the killer involving horses and a white dog. (My friend Bob Ussery witnessed Bob kill a horse and his involvement with Sirhan who was always around horses. Bob also owned a beautiful white Samoyed dog that everyone in Sunol admired).

The words Roth and Field, and a picture of a small bridge nine miles south of town flashed into DeLouise's mind, but he was unable to tell what meaning they had in solving the riddle of Zodiac's identity (Roth Field could be at Roth Air Base in West Germany where Bob abruptly landed his plane (like he did at Fort Lewis) and was detained. The driveway to Bob's place on Pacheco Road in Martinez is about nine miles from Vallejo at a small railroad bridge and there is a small narrow bridge in front of 187 Kilkare Road in Sunol.

In San Francisco, De Louise was not allowed to touch any of the physical evidence from the Stine case and came up with no impressions (DeLouise may have focused on Bob when Tom Pain was actually the perpetrator in this case).

Opening Greysmith's book was like falling down an elevator shaft the feeling made me physically ill and brought back all these terrible memories. I threw up in a trash can and was released from jury duty. I went to Sunol to post the SFPD Wanted Poster on the bulletin board near the post office so friends who knew both Bob and Tom could see it.

The first person I saw was Tom's older brother, Gerald. He hugged and thanked me for not testifying against Tom in Maryland. He said, "it would have killed my mother, Bob has him all fucked up in the head, it's day to day with Tom." That evening I saw Mike Hayner walk past my house up Foothill. I called him over and we spoke for a while, he showed me a nickel plated 357 Smith and Wesson that he had in his waist band and he stated, "I'm going to kill, Tom he is the Zodiac! We went camping at Lake Berryessa in September 1969 him and Hemphill took off on his motorcycle. I had to drive the white Chevy back to Sunol. There was a white small door in the trunk and when I got home it was gone. Tom raped his own daughters, did you know that?"

July 16, 1987: I was speaking with Nelson Crosby in front of 46 Kilkare Road in Sunol when Bob Hemphill stopped by in his diesel pickup. Bob would only talk about fishing and would not make eye contact with me. He only stayed for a few minutes and when he left, Nelson told me that he was going to work for Bob at his place in Martinez.

Nelson and I drove up to 211 Kilkare to see Bob's neighbor, there was this ad in the Independent Classified about some cars he had for sale.

As I drove into the yard I noticed through all the pine trees around Bob's house that between both houses there is only one address sign post 211 Kilkare (Bob's address is actually 187 Kilkare). Near Bob's house there was a sign on a gate that read Sierra. There were cars everywhere, many of them were sitting there rotting away with those kinds of temporary roof racks and some had camping gear stored in them.

The owner of the property, Joe Michael Hemovich, approximately sixty years old, 5'8, 175 lbs., walked up and saw us looking at Bob's house. I asked if he knew his neighbor Bob. (From audio tape) Joe asked:

"What about him?" I asked him how long he knew him. "Since I moved here several years ago, what's the deal with him anyway? Years ago he shot at the girl I used to rent to, she was on my property with a friend and he opened up on them for no reason. I couldn't believe it. I thought they were giving me bullshit, I didn't believe them. 'That's ridiculous,' she said, we were sitting there and bullets were hitting all around us. I asked if they were sure it was Bob Hemphill."

"They knew him! They said it was him! One day a couple years ago I was watering the trees on my property and pretty soon I heard a gun go off, bullets were hitting the tree and limb above my head, the branch came down and I hollered at him, he said something I couldn't understand.

I don't know, he fired a couple times. He liked to shoot BOOM, BOOM, BOOM you could hear him repeating with the .22. He's full of many different kinda guys; ya know he had the hots for the girl? He was around here all the time when she was here. And he shot at me; I knew she was telling the truth. I asked if it was two girls he shot at? no it was the girl and a boy. I asked them what they were doing, they said 'we were just sitting there and he started shooting.' She said that's the truth -she was a short girl, had a Karman Ghia just like mine, she had a funny name, I can't think of it now. I used to hear like a baby or kids crying over there. I don't know maybe from another house but it sure sounded like it was from over there a crying or something." I asked Joe if this was all the cars he had for sale. "No, I have an old Nash and Studebakers over near the Sunol golf course." We drove to the other locations; it was very close to where Jimmy burned to death.

When I saw the old Nash, it brought back memories of the wreck and fire on Pleasanton-Sunol Road. Behind a pile of wood I saw Gene Cesar's light green 1947 Studebaker (LMV144-BV #7GW3). I asked Joe where he got it, "I don't have paper on that and would give it to anyone that bought the 1950 Studebaker Commander." (KZU572- deteriorating blue spray can job over gray paint). I asked what was wrong with the 47 Studebaker. "it doesn't have a motor."

About a week later, I saw Nelson Crosby in town, "He is a weird guy all right he has these piles of woman's and little kid' clothes (panties and underwear) lying around his house. I found a crazy letter on the floor at his place in Martinez except for that his house is neat. The letter was on yellow lined paper it. It was all crumpled up and had a large stain on it. It looked exactly like the writing on some of the Zodiac letters." Nelson also said that the house in Martinez had a full basement. I asked what it was like, "it was flooded. He wouldn't write me a check! He had his brother do it." Bob told Nelson that he couldn't read or write. I called the Alameda County Sheriff's Department and Deputy Sheriff Garth Ludwig came out and took a report. I also showed him the SFPD wanted poster and senior yearbook pictures from Amador Valley High School in Pleasanton. He agreed it looks like them. Ludwig took the poster with yearbook pictures and the letter. I also showed him the cars at 211 Kilkare and at the golf course. Ludwig spoke with Joe about the cars and questioned him about the ownership.

July 12, 1987: I sent Bob Hemphill the following letter he mistook it be a death threat:

> FROM: DAVID SILVEY
> TO: Bob Hemphill
> RE: ZODIAC MURDERS
>
> As you know there is a contract out on me and probably also now realize that there is one on you. As you probably also realize that I am the only person left in the world that knows about the truth, that Zodiac was a cover for the CIA operations and that Tom fucked every thing up by going a killing spree. I was proud to work under you in the CIA in Frankfurt West Germany.
>
> I think you should tell the world the truth about the RFK hit, that it was actually a CIA hit. That you were hired to plan and carry it out. The FBI already knows all the details. I told them years ago

at Aberdeen Proving Grounds after Tom killed the woman at the train station.

The FBI also knows about the operation in Germany, they know all about the weapons that I signed for under CIA authority, because it was a CIA operation. Up to now they have kept their hands off, what would the world have thought of the government if they knew the truth? If they knew that you planned and Cesar actually did the killing.

Mel Belli had promised to represent you in court. You know now that and thanks to me the government has a completed record of what really took place. That we were working for the CIA and that you lost control of Tom and he destroyed and distorted the true image of what Zodiac was really about. This may have helped conceal the CIA operations and hits but it also tied you into taking the blame for his chicken shit murders.

I was proud to serve under you as a mercenary, but ashamed to be associated with what Tom did and is doing. He is talking about turning himself in; if he does you are going to take the blame. I hope you read in the newspapers about a new investigation into the RFK murder; that's what it's all about Bob Tom is turning on you and you are going to get the blame for all his shit while he gets amnesty for testifying against you.

Turn yourself over to me and tell the truth, I'll back you up and Mel Belli will defend you. Call me late at night 415-487-3422. Call before they make the hit on you or me. This is your last chance to clear yourself. You are guilty of losing control of your men not killing little girls in Santa Rosa!

July 26, 1987 Commerce Secretary Malcolm Baldridge dies in Rodeo accident:

I am sad to hear about Malcolm Baldridge [the Federal investigator] I am certain he is the reason I'm still alive. Baldridge protected me at the most dangerous time – when he visited me at Aberdeen Proving Grounds. The

CIA was through with me and I was talking too much at the Human Engineering Laboratory. Malcolm Baldridge calmed things down. He then got me transferred to the Ballistics Laboratory where I test fired and cleaned silenced M16's. Ironically he died at the Roddy Ranch in Brentwood,Ca.

Trying to get them out of circulation

August 1, 1987, I spoke with Lt. Lehman at the Vallejo Police Department and turned over much of the information on herein. He put it on top of a large stack of papers and files and said "Somebody will get back to you".

October 1987: I caught up with Bob at a phone booth near Big Daddy's Restaurant in Niles. I waited until he was off the phone then walked up while he was still in the booth. I confronted him about the RFK assassination and Gene Cesar. He had a terrified look on his face, his legs gave out from under him and he slides down the glass to the cement floor making kind of a weird scream. The glass panel pushed up his T-shirt and I could see an executioners tattoo. (heart with arteries severed). People were starting to stare and he had his feet against the doors so I left. Copies of information I turned over to the Sheriff's Department were now in Bob's hands and he showed it to several people in town this was fine with me. I wanted everyone to see it. Shortly after I left Big Daddies (2-3 hours) Deputy Ludwig arrived at 46 Kilkare and I asked if he spoke with Bob.

Bob can't read or write so he has other people read stuff to him, some people can't read and that's not against the law. I asked how Bob could be an electrician. He is smart enough to pull that off. Ludwig advised me that the letter I sent to Bob could be considered a death threat sent through the mail and that this was against the law. Ludwig further warned for me to leave Bob alone.

January 9.1988: A few months later, my beeper goes off and it's a 911 page from Nelson Crosby. I drove to 46 Kilkare and went inside then waited for Nelson to show up. (From audio tape) Nelson arrived, "Check this out, he [Bob Hemphill] has a cozy house, he has a cozy house. I slept with him, I helped him move, I slept with him, and he had a big boner! He told me you know everything, he said you are weird, you are a piece of shit!" Nelson asked for a ride up the canyon. We got into my car and as we passed Bob's house he turned and stared at me with a face full of hate. Nelson broke my windshield out with his fist, opened the door and rolled out onto the pavement. I made a U turn with the intention of running him over. As I got close enough to see the remorse on his face, I pulled up and yelled "Look what you did to my car asshole!" A bit of psycho circus in front of 187 Kilkare before Bob Hemphill and Tom Pain left Sunol for good.

January 13, 1989, Bob Hemphill parked in front of my home in his brown and tan diesel pick-up with a pop-up camper at 46 Kilkare Road in Sunol. He was throwing hard looks and we played the game several minutes until I surprised him with a camera.

Friday September 8 1989 I was shocked to hear of the attempted robbery of two Brinks guards at the Bank of America headquarters in the financial district:

When I heard the Messengers name "Joseph Arriola" I got sick to my stomach, I last saw him in the FBI's main lobby area at the Federal building in San Francisco. He was one of the Filipino Brink's SF vault men. My girl friend Michele Bauer, Arriola and I were waiting to be interviewed in connection with the Ukiah robbery.

The following is a Chronicle article by Susan Yoachum:

SAN FRANCISCO Two daring robbers who got away on brand new, bright blue ten speed bicycles continuing to elude police late Thursday after brutally slaying a Brinks security guard and seriously wounding another at the Bank of America world headquarters in the middle of the cities bustling financial district a third victim, bystander who was shot in the mouth when he tried to help the two guards, apparently will recover.

"The Brings guards didn't have a chance" said one witness, who said he arrive at that the scene about 5 seconds after the shooting." I didn't even think they saw who did it, it happened so fast," he said. "It was pretty grotesque".

The robbers, clawed in blue jean and golf caps and wearing ski masks, exalted with high fives before speeding away on their mountain bikes, careening from crowded sidewalks to busy streets. Police said their choice of a getaway vehicle was brilliant.

"Anytime you go down to the financial district during a busy day the best mode of transportation is a bicycle," said Whitey Guinther, Deputy Chief of the investigations.

Their getaway was clean, the gunmen apparently bungled there cold blooded heist. Police said the gunmen may have gotten no money- the Brinks guards may have been carrying only securities, bonds and travelers checks- and they could face the death penalty once they are caught.

The two men shot their victims with hand guns at pt blank range in a lobby just outside the Bank of America main branch. The guards, Joseph Arriola, 53 of Vallejo, and Clifford Spencer,24, of SF, a part time Brinks employee who started working for the company two and has months ago, was shot as they were leaving the main branch on California street. The third victim, Gardner Robert Lee, 57, of SF, was wounded after he rushed to the two guards, who he thought had stumbled and fallen on the way out of the bank.

Arreloa, a father of six, was shot in the head and was dead on arrival at SF General Hospital. Spencer, who was shot near the left eye brow remains in serious but stable condition at the hospital. Gee was in fair and stable condition.

Brinks incorporated offered a Hundred thousand dollar reward later in the day for information leading to the apprehension and conviction of the gunmen.

The getaway bikes were recovered in an alley near Market St. at 2:30pm, leading to speculation that the robbers continued their escape on public transit. Law enforcement officials and workers inside the busy B of A headquarters were stunned by the audacity of the bloody attack, which took place just before 10:00am.

"You really don't think people would have the nerve to pull something like that off," said Robert Birsinger, who works at the smoke shop in the same lobby where the shooting occurred.

The FBI spokesmen Chuck Latting, whose agency is aiding the SF police because the offense was a bank robbery, described the hold up as something." I never seen in twenty year in this office It sound like to me a real amateur operation" Latting said "Pros don't go in shooting, they know that's the death penalty. They hit the guards after they made the delivery, not before they did not have any money Latting said "None of that rings true to me"

San Francisco police, however, were not so sure the job was the work of amateurs." We don't know until we solve the case," said deputy chief Larry Gurnett.

One witness tracked the gunmen's route for several blocks before losing them on the busy financial district streets. The two were believed to have ridden down California Street, south on Montgomery to Bush, then east on Bush to Samsome.

"They lost them at that point," Latting said.

At a packed news conference late Thursday at the hall of justice, police inspectors appealed for help from the thousand financial district workers and Seers who might have witnessed the getaway. SF police set up a special hotline to accept tips on the case.

"There are just so many people down there. These guys traveled through tens of thousands people within a few blocks," said police captain John Newlin.

Police described one of the suspects as standing six foot two, weighing two hundred lbs. and being in his early thirties. The second suspect was believe to be in his 20"s.

"Both men are white."

Latting said "the streets surrounding the 52 story bank headquarters were quickly saturated with about 100 police officers and FBI agents, nearby Bart stations also were searched."

Law enforcement officials kept coming up dry until they got a tip about the bicycles on Thursday afternoon. But the bikes apparently had been ditched on Ecker alley shortly after10:00am., according to the person who tipped the police more than four later.

The shooting took place just down the lobby from the smoke shop, were co-owner Judy Adami mistook shots for breaking glass. Just then a bloody man came stumbling toward her candy and newsstand.

"I heard these noises: I thought one of the glass cases had broken," she said." Just then a man came running over clutching his mouth with both hands. I said, what happened? He just said," There's been a robbery I've been shot, I'm hurt and his teeth were all out."

RECONCILING THE EVIL

March 7, 1999, I spoke with Darlene Ferrin's younger sister, Pam Huckaby:

It has been thirty years since I last saw Pam at the 1969 painting party in Vallejo. Pam said, "a man that bothered Darlene for the last 2 years of her life killed someone and Darlene saw it". Pam was excited and sincerely convinced that I was onto something, in fact she quoted from her diary a passage about us showing up at the party. "There were three young men who were so strange that they made Karen so uncomfortable that she left the house."

I sent Pam the high school yearbook pictures of Bob Hemphill and Tom Pain to Pam.

On March 9, 1999 Pam got the pictures and was very upset, "It was a tough night sleeping, but I managed somehow. I do remember Bob, but his hair was thicker and longer somewhat, as I think back on that night he stayed for a while, I don't remember when he left. I think he was still there when someone took me home. I think he had a light colored sweater. If I can pick out the man that bothered Darlene at Terry's I know Bob is the guy, in the kitchen leaning up against a table."

On May 16, 2001, I received a call from Sirhan's attorney Lawrence Teeter. Larry told me that "his stomach was in knots" after reading the letter that I had sent him about a week earlier that described the events, that I witnessed that took place before the assassination. Larry requested more information and I was glad to send it. I was shocked and disheartened when I learned of his death.

On July 4, 2002, I spoke with Leo Suennen at Blue Rock Springs in Vallejo, the site of his sister's murder thirty three years ago. Leo remembered me from the painting party. Leo stated that Darlene used the cross tops herself or gave them away to friends, She never sold them. I asked Leo why Mike was wearing three layers of clothes that summer night. Leo said, "He needed to get blood off, I think he was going to shed layers of clothes to get Darlene's blood off. I saw Darlene an hour before they came out here and she was fine, they both got set up."

A few days later I met White Rabbit at All Stars Donuts on Mission Street in San Francisco and we spoke for about an hour. I asked him if he remembers me. So I said "I used to sell you acid." He said, "That's right." I then asked if he remembers where we were the last time we saw each other. "I was working at the Straight Theater you and your buddy didn't like the show." I asked Rabbit if he remembers the guy with the gun running after us. "I don't remember that but I remember shots being fired right after you guys left out the exit."

I asked Rabbit about Charlie's miracles?

"We were on the bus at the Spiral Staircase and we had dropped acid. We had just had a family orgy, when Clem, who was cutting wax off a candle with a razor blade, missed and sliced his dick off. There was blood everywhere and Clem's dick was on the mattress. Charlie then laid hands on Clem's head and said "Heal me." Miraculously Clem's dick flew up and reattached itself and all the blood disappeared. We got on our hands and knees and bowed our heads and said "Praise God our Father healed him." It was a sign that Jesus had returned.

The next miracle happens in the woods of Ukiah while we were on acid in the bus during the witches of Mendocino Trial. Mother Mary went into the woods to take a shit, came running back like a bat out of hell. She was being chased by a 600 pound grizzly bear. Facing sure death Charlie leaped out of the bus and looked that bear in the eyes. The bear was standing straight up and he gave the bear a pure old fashioned grin.

The bear stopped in his tracks and Charlie kept grinning. Charlie saw the bear back down, Charlie petted it and told Mother Mary to give him our honey and extra table scraps and Charlie let the bear eat out of his hand. We did not have room in the bus or else we would have taken the killer bear traveling with us. Charlie's eyes were hypnotic, they could be very gentle or they could actually be terrifying."

Cartoon like in nature, Manson's operational use of LSD and hypnosis for deliberate insertion of false memories. After 36 years White Rabbit believes Charlie Manson is Jesus and for all intents and purposes he and would be assassins Sara Jane Moore and Squeaky Froamme are still ARTICHOKED! By Manson?

On July 10, 2002, I received a reply to my Freedom of Information Act request concerning any records or files the CIA may have in my name along with dates and places. I had contact with the agency to aid them in the search.

Central Intelligence Agency

Washington, D.C. 20505

10 July 2002

Mr. David M. Silvey
1630 N. Main St. #188
Walnut Creek, CA 94596

Reference: P-2002-00429

Dear Mr. Silvey:

This acknowledges receipt of your letter dated 22 May 2002 (received here 10 June 2002) wherein you requested information pertaining to yourself. For identification purposes we have assigned your request the reference number above.

As you may know, the discovery of anthrax in a letter mailed to the United States Senate on October 15 led to a series of escalating safety concerns about opening, handling, and even being in the proximity of mail, especially in government offices in Washington, D.C. These concerns, in turn, led to disruptions in, and then total curtailments of, mail delivery service, to include Freedom of Information Act-related correspondence, at many federal agencies, including the Central Intelligence Agency.

Under such extraordinary circumstances, the administration of the Freedom of Information Act has inevitably been delayed at all affected federal agencies. As a matter of both common sense and legal precedent, when mail delivery is delayed, so is the commencement of the process of FOIA administration, regardless of the time at which a FOIA request is placed into the mail by the requester or postmarked thereafter. Simply put, the FOIA process cannot begin until the personnel of an agency FOIA office are able to open any belatedly delivered item of mail.

To the extent that you seek records that might reveal a covert connection between you and the CIA, I must advise you that in all requests such as yours, the CIA can neither confirm nor deny the existence or nonexistence of any CIA records responsive to your request. The fact of the existence or nonexistence of records containing such information--unless, of course, it has been officially acknowledged--would be classified for reasons of national security under Sections 1.3(a)(4) [intelligence sources and methods] and 1.3(a)(5) [foreign relations] of Executive Order 12958. Further, the Director of Central Intelligence has the responsibility and authority to protect such information from unauthorized disclosure in accordance with Subsection 103(c)(6) of the National Security Act of 1947 and Section 6 of the CIA Act of 1949.

Therefore, to the extent your request might concern records containing such information, it is denied pursuant to Freedom of Information Act exemptions (b)(1) and (b)(3) and Privacy Act exemptions (j)(l) and (k)(l). An explanation of these exemptions is enclosed. By this action we are neither confirming nor denying that any such information exists.

You have the right to appeal this determination by addressing your appeal to the Agency Release Panel, in my care. Your appeal, however, cannot be accepted until we have completed all processing on your request at which time you can appeal any denials within 45 days from the date of our final response letter.

We will search for any other information pertaining to you, including that which might reflect an open or otherwise acknowledged Agency affiliation. Since you have provided the necessary information, we have accepted the remaining portion of your request. It will be processed in accordance with the Freedom of Information Act (FOIA), 5 U.S.C. § 552, as amended, and the Privacy Act of 1974, 5 U.S.C. § 552a. Our search will be for documents in existence as of and through the date of this acceptance letter. No fees will be charged.

The heavy volume of FOIA requests received by the Agency has created delays in processing. Since we cannot respond within the 20 working days stipulated by the FOIA, you have the right to consider this a denial and may appeal to the Agency Release Panel. It would seem more reasonable, however, to have us continue processing your request and respond to you as soon as we can. You can appeal any denial of records at that time. Unless we hear from you otherwise, we will assume that you agree, and we will proceed on this basis.

Sincerely,

Chris K.

for Kathryn I. Dyer
Information and Privacy Coordinator

Enclosure

October 20, 2002, I sent a letter to Inspector Michael Maloney of the San Francisco Police Department Homicide Section. In the letter to Inspector Maloney, I put together a short synopsis of my key points regarding Zodiac for consideration in respect to the investigation. May 24, 1969 at a friend's request, we attended a party with Bob Hemphill at 1300 Virginia Street in Vallejo. The fourth Zodiac victim, Darlene Ferrin, knew 'Bob well', as 'Bob', and he was the man harassing her at the party. He talked us into coming under false pretense and we left after a minor incident, but Bob stayed. In the fall of 1970 Tom Pain bragged that he left the city covered in the cabdriver's blood. Bob never got close enough to the scene to be noticed and had no blood on his clothing when a few minutes later two patrolman drove up. The composite poster generated later by witness accounts was incredibly accurate on both men. Most believe it to be an amended composite of one man Zodiac. For comparison I enclosed a copy of the 1989 SFPD Wanted poster with Tom Pain's 1964 senior yearbook picture both from Amador Valley High School in Pleasanton.

October 22, 2002, Inspector Maloney sent a reply to my letter requesting that I call between 8:00 am and 10:00 am. I called and spoke with Inspector Maloney who asked several questions concerning my key points.

He stated that the 1969 SFPD Wanted Poster with Tom Pain's 1964 senior yearbook picture and Bob Hemphill's 1955 senior yearbook picture didn't look like the composite to him, but he would contact Bob and Tom, and then get together with his partner and be in touch.

Zodiac Case File Shut

April 7, 2004: Front page San Francisco Chronicle: FILES SHUT ON ZODIAC'S DEADLY TRAIL, SFPD caseload rendered the 25 year mystery inactive.

"It has been one of the longest, most famous and frustrating homicide investigations in San Francisco, and haunting detectives for more than 35 years. Now, just two years after DNA evidence suggested that a break might come soon, police have "deactivated" the case of the Zodiac Killer.

"The case is being placed inactive," said San Francisco police Lt. John

Hennessey, who heads the department's homicide unit. "Given the pressure of our existing caseload and amount of cases that remain open at this time, we need to be most efficient at using our resources."

Homicide inspectors are under increasing pressure to solve a rash of gang- and drug-related killings in the city. Mayor Gavin Newsom has shown up at some crime scenes and recently suggested that the department's success rate needed serious improvement.

The move to shut down the case means that, for the first time, no inspector will be assigned to actively investigate the case or follow up leads unless an extraordinary tip comes in. As a result, the trail of the Zodiac- who is blamed for committing at least five brazen murders in 1968 and 1969 that terrified the Bay Area and who reveled in sending taunting letters to police and newspapers – appears colder than ever.

"The police shall never catch me, because I have been too clever for them", the Zodiac, predicted almost 35 years ago in a letter sent to The Chronicle. "I enjoy needling the blue pigs," he wrote later in the same letter.

According to Hennessey, the case had been put on hold several times over the past few decades.

Now, however, three decades' worth of evidence has been locked away in a battered gray file cabinet kept in a closet across from the department's cramped homicide office. There are no plans to unlock it.

The following Napa Sentinel article by Harry V. Martin reports why the 35 year Zodiac Killer investigation may have failed:

NAPA SENTINEL "At least one law enforcement investigator of the Zodiac has admitted that the search for the Zodiac killer never focused on the victims and their backgrounds. Believing the Zodiac to be a random serial killer, police never sought to determine if any of the victims were related. If the victims had a relationship with each other, it would indicate that the Zodiac was not a crazy wanton killer, but a person who killed his victims to prevent them from revealing information.

The Zodiac letters did not appear until after Ferrin was killed yet Ferrin was murdered in 1969. The first victim linked to the Zodiac was murdered in 1966, and two more in 1968. Why the delay in claiming credit for the murders? The first phone call the police received from the Zodiac was after Ferrin's murder there were no phone calls associated with the other three murders.

Ferrin also apparently knew her assailant according to several witnesses, including Michael Mageau, who was shot along side of Ferrin on July 4, 1969. Numerous reports refer to a man in middle age wearing horn rimmed glasses and driving a white vehicle as the man Ferrin was afraid of who had come to her home and to her work frequently. He was a man she drove around at least once, and a man who attended her house painting party though he was not invited. He was the man Ferrin said she saw kill a man. He was the man who brought her boxes of material, silver buckles and perhaps thousands of dollars.

Ferrin is the key to solving the Zodiac murders. But she is also the key to proving that the Zodiac was a hoax. He was not a random killer, he killed for a purpose. Ferrin knew too much, she had apparently witnessed a murder and because she was always meeting with this man, and arguing with him, and he was bringing her packages, she and he had some arrangement. Ferrin admitted to being afraid of him yet she still associated with him. He sat outside her home on numerous occasions. He ate strawberries in Vallejo at Terry's Restaurant, where she worked. She did not want any of her family members talking with this man, he was too dangerous. The man wore a medical alert bracelet and was ambidextrous, smoked Pall Mall cigarettes, and wore horned rimmed glasses.

On the night of her murder, Ferrin had an argument with this man in a restaurant parking lot and, according to Mageau, the man followed them in his white car. Mageau, it must be noted has changed his story many, many times. After the murder Mageau went into hiding for over 20 years though it is believed that he was living in Southern California during his self-established exile. Mageau apparently knows who the killer is though he has not provided that information to the police.

Ferrin also knew Paul Stein (another Zodiac victim) very well, according to Ferrin's family. They both lived in a boarding house in San Francisco in late 1966, Stein apparently drove Ferrin around San Francisco frequently. She worked at the Pacific Telephone in San Francisco in 1966. Stein drove a Yellow Cab. Ferrin was murdered on July 4, 1969; Stein was murdered October 11, 1969 ninety nine days later. Ferrin was murdered by a man matching the description of the man who is believed to have killed Stein.

To understand the Zodiac, it is vital that the investigator understand Darlene Ferrin without knowledge of her lifestyle, the clue to the Zodiac would never be revealed.

Darlene knew a terrible secret and it is probably because of that secret she was murdered not randomly, but deliberately and with malice. The uninvited man who attended a painting party at Darlene's mingled with three Vallejo police officers who also were in attendance. Ironically, it was one of those officers, who would have seen the murderer face-to-face without realizing it, who was the first policeman on the scene of Darlene's shooting.

The suspect drove a light colored car during the time that Darlene knew him, and the day after she was murdered, he traded the car in at San Francisco auto dealer.

But let us trace the history of Darlene Ferrin, who she was and what happened to her. Darlene lived in Vallejo and graduated from Hogan High School. After graduation she went to San Francisco to work with the telephone company.

Darlene lived in a boarding house-type facility. According to Darlene's family, that boarding house or resident hotel was on Eddy Street. Also briefly living there was Paul Stine, a yellow Cab driver who was a claimed Zodiac victim. The suspect was associated with the residential hotel in San Francisco on Eddy Street. Darlene's first husband was a resident of the residential hotel. It was through this facility, that Darlene met Michael Mageau, the man who was also shot on the night of July 4, 1969.

Stine later moved to Cole Street in the Haight-Ashbury, Darlene and her husband moved to Vallejo. Mageau also moved to Vallejo and the Zodiac suspect eventually moved to Balboa Street in San Francisco.

Though Darlene was into the occult and may have belonged to a satanic or witch coven, it was probably not the reason for her death. Whatever she practiced in the occult she did not seem to take the entire thing seriously. However her practice in the coven was associated with San Francisco and not necessarily Vallejo. A robe similar to those used in rituals associated with these organizations was found in the back of her closet in San Francisco by a family member. There has been a lot of speculation concerning satanic associations with the Zodiac, particularly since his letters are suggestive in that manner. But it is possible that Darlene did have an association with several people intertwined in the Zodiac investigation that participated in similar rites. But all the trails associated with coven relate to San Francisco and not Vallejo.

Was Darlene into drugs and money laundering? Her associations with the Crocker bank and her late entrance into money cast a suspicion on the legitimacy of her activities. Darlene used layaway plans and did not buy expensive clothes, she only had her salary as a waitress.

She was generally chubby and wore braces, but in the last months of her life, she lost a lot of weight, became very attractive and suddenly could afford very expensive clothes and jewelry at least expensive compared to her former lifestyle. She was able to purchase a home, but strangely enough that house was under her name and her father-in-law's name not her husband's. Though Darlene was married a second time, she was anticipating a divorce and commenced to date other men, including several police officers. She was very outgoing and friendly.

She had one frequent caller, a man who made her very nervous. He was a man that she warned her family not to talk with. She said she witnessed this man kill someone. Was the person Cheri Jo Bates in Riverside on October 30, 1966 the night of a satanic ritual? The answer to that question appears to be no. The man who may have killed Darlene and shot Mageau, was known by the two victims. The man also had only half a smile because part of his face was partially paralyzed from a cement truck accident. He was 41-years-old at the time. He had short curly, light brown hair in a crew cut style and a round face. The man was about 195 pounds and about five feet eight inches tall.

The suspect brought presents to Darlene's house, including cloth for a dress, a silver buckle and what is believed to be money. The packages were generally left on the doorstep of Darlene's house, but on one occasion her sister was given the package. Her sister had visited with the man at Terry's restaurant in Vallejo where Darlene worked, and he was at a painting party at Darlene's home

Darlene is quoted as stating the following to her sister on February 27, 1969, one hundred twenty seven days before she was killed: "I guess he's checking up on me again. I heard he was back from out of state. He doesn't want anyone to know what I saw him do. I saw him murder someone." Another quotation on Saturday, December 21, 1968, the day after David Faraday and Betty Lou Jenson were murdered on Lake Herman Road: "This is scary, I knew the two kids who were killed on Lake Herman Road. Yeah, I'm not going up there again."

Darlene changed emotionally after the Faraday-Jenson murderers. People close to her noticed nervousness, a concern. She was scared of the man in the horn-rimmed glasses after he returned from out of state in February 1969. She didn't want people near him, she was not too friendly with him, yet he hung around her, brought her presents and lavished his affections on her. We know she was afraid of him because she witnessed a murder he committed, according to her own words. But it was murder she did not report and yet she had many friends who were police officers. The suspected murderer also knew Mageau because of past relationships in San Francisco and also through his contacts with Darlene.

When Jenson and Faraday were found dead, on Lake Herman road shot to death. The heater in their car was still on and yet the window was rolled down on that cold December night. This suggests that a conversation between the people in the killer's car and the victims had taken place. No one claimed credit for the Jenson and Faraday murders not at the time. But after Darlene's murder, the Zodiac took credit for both sets of killings.

One senior police officer not related directly to the case, but who has conducted an extensive investigation on the Zodiac, suggests that Darlene was with the Zodiac suspect on Lake Herman Road on December 20, 1968, and that Darlene may have had a conversation with Jenson at the scene. The murder that Darlene would have witnessed, according to this veteran police officer, would have been Faraday. She had indicated she saw a man killed. Jenson fled the scene and was shot outside the immediate vicinity of the victim's vehicle.

Darlene had indicated that a big story would break in the newspapers around July 5, 1969 a really big story. She related that in the same context as the information about witnessing the murder. What was Darlene talking about? It is believed that she was going to expose this man for the murder she saw him commit. There are no records that indicate she went to the police or to the newspaper - but the threat was there. She had an argument with the suspect in the restaurant parking lot hours before she was killed and the suspect followed her and Mageau to the scene where they were both shot'. (Harry V. Martin)

October 31, 2006: At midnight I left a message on Bob's answering machine: an offer for Hemphill to write the final chapter. Bob called back several times, repetitively hanging up, and using up all the message tape with silence.

March 4, 2008 Bob Hemphill: [from audio tape]

> Yeah… him and Dave were hav-… had something going on when they lived in Sunol. And… that's when the book got put in my… truck.

> Back then… we had bought a… my brother-in-law and I bought a place in Pacheco and that's how Dave got involved in it…

> Besides the twelve acres up on the side of the hill there…

> The railroad washed out, the bank washed out. Anyway that's where my brother bought… we bought it from uhhh…

> …what was his name…. He was a contractor, what did he do? I gotta… but anyway… I was up there cleanin' the place up for my brother… I was all… in this… and had time, and had room up there and my brother's a general contractor. So we were up there

cleanin' the place up and I remember we had a guy up there that uh... was a Green Beret, a Captain I think he was.

...where did it go wrong and a lot of stuff that's intermittent to it where all the stuff that happened along the way. He was living up there... and I got to know him, but not really well... and I wanted him out of there. I wanted him out of there... so I could clean the place up. He was a character... I think he was a Captain and he was uh... kinda' like a soldier of fortune like. ...they set 'em up anythin' to do...

...with killin' stuff. And he was... he got He hit a Captain. He was tellin' me that...

He hit a Captain and he went back in to uh... with a helicopter... in, was it Afghanistan or somewhere? And they went in and they did a mockup of this... to... to retrieve one of the... one of the uh... soldiers.

I mean this is weird... I mean this is the stuff that happened while all this other stuff was goin' on... and anyway he was tellin' me about. But anyway... uh... the helicopter got... when they seen him, I can't remember who was in that... when they sent the helicopter. And the guy that was flyin' the helicopter was a Senator's son that was a Captain or somethin' and then those bastards... oh my god. And he got them killed. That's what it was. He was... the guy that was livin' where I was cleanin' up was tellin' me you know, little bits and pieces. And then uh... I guess he cold-cocked him, and he got off of the case... so anyway... so that... And the next thing was Marcos. They had a hit on Marcos... that he was supposed to go in and assassinate him.

...he was military... like a seal... and I mean... and he lived in there and there were fleas all over the place. I couldn't stand it in there... I thought Ken they was crawlin' all over me and he was sleepin' in that crap. And he slept with a knife. He carried a 9 mm. And I uh... found some cases, and I found the knife, ya' know. But he always... and he slept in the raw and kinda' rough to sleep in the raw all the time. Anyway I had a really big case tryin' to get rid of him… it was… you know I had to watch out 'cause it scared me. I didn't know what his capability was… so I was kinda'…

You know… yeah… Then we had a tenant up there and I got into trouble with that… they made calls… They were just different and they were pretty ornery… and I was kinda' young ya' know… and I'd just come out and I'd say how it was. And nobody likes that… nobody liked to be told you're an asshole.

So… So… Well anyway… you know, but… but Dave came to help… I… I needed some help and Nelson came up to help me. He lived at the end of the canyon. And uh… him and… I didn't know that him and Dave were buddies… not at the time. So anyway… uh… he worked for me…

…oh maybe a couple days… I got him three… three or four days helped out cleanin' up ya' know… and he needed a few bucks ya' know… and we helped him out. And then… I lived there on the other side of the church and I come down and get in my… was that a Chevie down there it was… a Chevie yeah… anyway… I get down there… and I looked down and I seen that book sittin' there on the side…

… And I seen that uh… that… the Zodiac book. I checked it out… what the hell… I didn't put that there… what the hell… I kinda' opened it up and I looked – you look at the composite have you ever seen that book? You look at the… You get that… You get that… You get that paperback book and you open it up… and I looked at him and I go "Son of a bitch… it looks like me…". Burned the shit out of me.

That's when the stuff started snowballing and kinda' movin' along… and I had no idea how… where it was gonna' go… how far it was gonna' go and whatever end… or… and like I said uh… Nelson is gay. And Davey I think… him and Davey were having something… they… they… they… ok.

They broke his windshield. He broke Dave's windshield. He smashed it. He got mad at him. Nelson broke Davey's windshield down there in Sunol. He put his fist through it. They got in an argument about somethin'. But Dave... or Nelson was drunk... and he was drunk. And he kept... he talked to me two or three nights later or whatever it was. And he kept.. and he started talking to me and I give him a ride up the road... and he goes "You're the zzzzzzz..." And he kept going "You're the zzzzz..." I said "What?" And he said "You're the zzzzz..."

He couldn't get it out. It scared him. He didn't know. And he put everything to where I lived... in Vallejo, right across the Bay. And then the composite... the picture of mine... with the glossies that I had at that time... and then just the profile. A straight ahead shot. I looked at that and I go "Holy fuck..." And I started stuff, and I started thinking about it. So Dave... But I mean other... other than just a picture of me... he spooked me.

And then... then Nelson comes up and he's over to here "You're the zzzzz" "You're the zzzzz" So anyway, he was in my truck and finally I said "What the hell are you tryin' to say?" He said "You're the ZZZZ... You're the Zodiac killer..." And I said "What the hell are you talkin' about?" And man... my wheels started turnin'. And he started comin' on to me. I had a huntin' knife settin' in the side compartment over here. He reached over and he started grabbin' my leg. And I says "If you don't take your friggin hand off my leg..." I says "I don't go for this kind of crap... I'm gonna cut your hand off. I'll cut it off right now. I'm not like that. If you and Silvey wanta' pull that kinda' crap that's fine with me. I don't care what you do. But don't get me involved in it." Now somehow he just... he feathered off and kinda' went into the sunset. Then the next thing I heard... was... uh... let's see what did I do... I got the letter...

When I got the letter... in the mail... then I went to the... uh... I talked to the airline pilot which is... he lived there in Sunol... uh. Anyway... yeah... anyway he uh... he started talking to me. And he says… "You don't want this thing out." So he says… uh… he said "I threw the book in the garbage can." So I went and grabbed it back. And then… uh… I had that and the letter, so it didn't get thrown away I think it was open to Pachecko? And I remember you know where the scales are there on 680 past the golf course in Sunol, the Sunol golf course, the scales on the left side and you go up there's a frontage road. There's a area up there, a cul-de-sac at the end of the road. I met the sheriff up there and I talked to him… for… a couple hours.

And uh… Anyway the deal with the Zodiac guy, the crimpt and whatever he was doing… He's a smart fucker. He… he… he really was. And… and the airlines pilot… can't think of his name… "Frank ain't smart enough to do that." You know that… you know the… No. But he… he says… whatever… I can't even explain what he was… when he'd go after somebody and kill 'em. He'd do somethin' with letters… astrology or some damn thing. And I never did quite understand that. But anyway… it's kind of comical. And… and uh…

…the uh… I think that's what it was. Yeah. And I go what the hell is that anyway. And I had no… and I'm goin' through the book just kinda'… I just scan… scanned through it and I seen some of the stuff in there. I got a kick outa' the airlines pilot he told the cop, he says "Frank ain't that smart." He says "He's a good electrician but he ain't that smart." And I kinda' laughed and I goes "I don't even know what the hell they're talking about." You know… and it was kinda' comical at that. But… I… I… I was scared and then the deal about him bein' on the roof and I shot at him.

Yep… he was… I don't know if it was in Sunol or what. And kinda' right after that… this just kinda' went on for about 2 - 3 weeks… I… what the hell… I didn't know… I didn't know Silvey. …" I says, "…what's goin' on with Silvey?" I said, "Man he got some weird friggin ideas." And I said "You know I never…". You know I told him about Germany and I says "I never been there." I says "… and being affiliated with us dealing in weapons and all." I says "Man this is high tech stuff..." I says, "It's way over my head... I have no idea what's goin' on." And I said "First off... you know I haven't been to Germany... when in the hell did I go over there that I didn't know about it?" So anyway... he kind of clued me in and he says... You know what... I'll tell you how... what I think how it started. Dave read the Zodiak killer book...

He read that paperback. And what he does... he reads that and the next thing you know he's affiliated whatever has gone on with that individual or whatever's in that book. He takes that on in his head. And... and... and he gets himself so involved in it.

Darleen? No. No... but I'll tell you what uh... As soon as all this stuff got... pretty disturbing it was gonna' come out on the news. And they said that the information... and this was right after I talked to the sheriff. So somehow that information got leaked out to the news media 'cause it came out that he had surfaced. ...

I don't... from what has happened with him, and what has happened, what he's done to me by his imagination... his figment of imagination. It put a mark on me that is not gonna' go away. And what scares me more than anything else is... is like I was tellin' you... there's a lotta' innocent people in jail who haven't done a thing. By association. And that disturbed the hell out of me when all this started... this stuff started goin'... And my brother, he got worried. And he told me And I had a... I HAD NO IDEA... I had no idea what he was gonna' do. Or how far he was...

Is what? I don't want to talk to him or get around him 'cause he... he's pissed me off. And I know his brain... how it starts workin' and it... I don't want it goin' in to anything else again... I've had enough of it. And you can see where it is right now. It's comin' back again. So he's doin' it again. And... ya know... and like I said, if uh... if I was that smart to be that individual I wouldn' be sittin' here right now.

Yeah... I mean it just... you know... I may be Italian but I'm not... I... I... can git things done. I can be an ornery son of a gun, and I mean I... I try to watch out for myself. I get... I'm very... uh... protective of myself in that sense when it comes back to him. It just... scares me to think... that... without have done anything... to put me another position that I don't want to be into.\You know... I had no idea when... when... when he was out there and you guys were out there. I told Tim... I told him I says "If that phone don't ring in... in ten minutes... if I don't call you back in ten minutes... you... you call... you call the Lieutenant... you call the lieutenant up there to pick my body up." 'Cause I have no idea..."and... uh... uh.

...uh... uh... I have no idea... uh... well I'd like to see what he's... I'd like... I'd like to... yeah... But like I s... that's what I'm trying... that's what I'm explainin'...is. He's just...

See I was... see I was right... on what I was thinkin' that he always thought hat I was that individual. And, and... 'cause this is what carried it off so far. But why... why... should he ever say "Frank and I went to Germany and we bought all these..." somethin' to that letter. Did you read the letter? I can't remember...

He sent me a letter in the mail... that the sheriff's department has it in uh... in Alameda County. They have that letter and they have the book. Now whether it's cold dead file or whatever it is... or whatever's goin' on. And like I said, I wanted to... [puckering sound]... get this to the sheriff's department to make sure that if anything went on, and I was above board, I gave 'em all the information, and if anything came back up, and they never ever come back to me... about... the Zodiiac killer. It did surface. It did come up. And I knew what was gonna' happen. and that's why I did what I did to cover my own butt. To say "Hey - this is what was happenin' on my end over here. I want you guy's to know. And if he comes over to you and starts talkin' to you and sayin' "Hey I think he's the Zodiac killer." Well I came to you guys first." And I covered... I covered...

Well I could'a come out there with a AR15 or somethin' like that and blown all of you away.

But I'll tell you right now I got a restrainin' order I can't have a weapon. On accounta' my neighbors, so you're lucky.

You're lucky... you're lucky the troopers didn't show up when you were there. I mean a... uh... see... Tim's off... on the other side 'a Redding. Traffic control. 'Cause I knew he was workin' overtime. And when I put the call in to him his phone was... I had a hard time gettin' back through 'cause he was on that phone callin' ALLLL the guys around tryin' to find out who's where, where they at. And then the...

Oh... they're illegal. And I mean he was a busy... and I really apologized to him for puttin' him through what I put him through, 'cause he was worried. He was scared for me.

Well... that's what the... what the founder of the mark and are now with all the stuff... all you gotta' do is get with the tappin'... you don't even have to be tapped anymore. They're... they're... That's right. And if you s... if that gets picked up like you said, it could open up another bucket 'a worms. And then you go "What the hell are those guys's dark suits down on my driveway over here. What's goin' on?"

Yeah... Well I wasn't...you know... it... like I say... Just gittin' started off we got off on the wrong foot 'cause I was pissed. I didn't know what was goin' on.

I didn't know if I was gonna' walk back in that house or not. And then... just what I say that I made some phone calls right off the bat... so... and then... 'cause he... Tim knew what was goin' on from before.

But uh... no it's just strange that this is opened up again. After this amount of ti[me]...

You're trying to get some information. You're trying to find out what the hell's goin' on. Really am I who he says I am.

You're get[ting]... and then... like I said... or like you said... if I was - you wouldn't have driven up that driveway. I'd 'a had this tractor runnin' and I woulda' dug a hole and seen him buried over there.

I mean... I mean... Because if... if I was worried... yeah... if I was worried I got a lotta' neighbors. And you know and I woulda' done more got license numbers and... and I wouldna' called Tim... I wouldna' called to say hey... uh... this 'n that... you know goin' on. Why... why would I do... why would I expose... stuff in front of this guy... you know.

It's a fig... it's not a story, it's a figment of his imagination that he read a book... and... and ... he... he read... he read the book and he got inside that book and that book got inside 'a his head. And it's... and it's like I said when I...

... I don't know if he'll be honest with you or what, but what he told me was that guy is... is... he just goes off tilt when he starts... When he gets on somethin' that is...IT.

Which I really didn't wanna' be... one of the characters by choice. I was kinda' drawn into it through Nelson. And... and... and... and... by... by... what drew me... well... what drew me into it was they look... no... he looked at that book and he seen the composite. That's where it all started. I fig'red that out a long time ago.

I was just tryin' to remember... Naw I think it was... remember what I was doin'. Uh... I think it was... I think it was before... '70...'70 something. Well... see I worked at... at Kaiser for 10 years. I left there in '76.

Kaiser Site for Technology that's no longer there in Pleasanton. They had a... a... aluminum de-... aluminum recycling... yeah. Brite... yeah and see there's another story. We... we had... when they put that plant there in Pleasanton, Spokane moved individuals down to Pleasanton. Rapes started across in the co-ed dorms and uh… across the college… yeah… across the Bay. The guy… I'll think of his name in a minute… he's up in uh Susanville right now. I don't think they every let him go. Carter. Carter was his name. Carter was his… No… no not Curlin Carter. Uh… his name was Carter. But he worked for GE and he… er uh worked for Kaiser and he came from uh… from uh… Spokane. And all this stuff started… all this stuff started surfacing… in… let's see when did I start at Kaiser… '60. But when I moved up here… and here's Carter's face with a big crosshairs on him. They were gonna' shoot him if they let him go. He was … he was… they caught him, they caught him… he was goin' around rapin' on women. Goin' into the dorms. Getting his jollies off. And I… I was an electrician… at uh Kaiser then. And I was sittin' there and I moved up an' I was lookin' an I said "God damn that's Carter." And they were gonna' let him go. And uh the sheriff's told 'em they says "We can't protect him." So they kept him. I don't know if he's still up there now or not. That was like six, six, eight years ago.

No I got… my stomach will go bonkers. No… the sauce in there. I gotta'… I gotta'… I gotta' bad tummy. Just a little bit. But uh… that's good.

I mean this is just some 'a the things that happened. You know… I mean that

Remember when he… I knew… well see I knew Postel and all that 'cause he was around there. Silvey… see I never did… yeah… I never did uh… I never did… really… socialize with Dave.

'Cause he… he just wasn't in my… he… he wasn't in my pathway… uh so to speak. He… he just wasn't… he just wasn't involved other than… I think… and all I knew him, and the name came off, was when he was workin' for his Dad. When they were makin' the ripper teeth. Or they make tool and die or whatever it was.

And he was pretty good dad was a real good tool and die guy…

It's a dog eat dog… world… dog eat dog, I'll tell ya'… sometimes… And I'm not gonna' get chewed up. I made… I made… I made my mind up a long time ago when all this…. I said I'm gonna' cover my butt. And that's why I did the things that I did knowin' how the judicial system works. Sometimes the judicial system doesn't work it breaks down.

And it… and it… you know… and it… just… and… and I… like I said I sat there and I thought about it and I told my brother… we were sittin' there talkin'. And I says "You know what?" I says "This just scares the hell out of me" I says "I'm gettin' blamed…" If you read the restrainin' order… If you read the restrainin' order that the guy wrote on me… and I stayed at the house the whole time I never confronted him. They came over to me… and I got crucified. That just goes to show you how… you know. And… and me like a dummie, I didn't say anything but I felt like a shit though. If I woulda' known what I'd known right now I would turned everything around on 'em. I had a… I had a… I had a restrainin' order that was against me and not her. And… I come that close to goin' to jail in that ballgame. She told me I tried to kill her… on the ridge.

So I mean… it's just… you know I mean… it's… uh… I mean… And from all this other… from all this other stuff that's goin' on I kinda' learned uh to protect myself… And… and I go… you know… and you just… and there… and… and there's… and there's… there's a lot of uh… individuals out there that'll… just to get… on that next stepping stone… to better themselves… like District Attorneys… they lie like hell. And they get something stuck in their head and they ain't gonna' let go of it. They're gonna' go "YOU DID IT."

That's right. Whether you did or not. They're not open minded. And… and the thing that bothers me is you turn around 10, 20 years later the guy got DNA proved they didn't do it. And they says "I told you… when you were lockin' me up that I didn't do it. And you set there and you were so headstrong sayin' that I did it." And

I was runnin'... I was runnin' that through my head while all this stuff was goin' on with me. And I go you gotta' cover yourself. You gotta'... you know... you get in there and make sure that...

They're... you know... you just... There's an onion... Oh the onions are ok.

Yeah. Well you know the thing that amazes me is... is that you... you come up here. And I'm sittin' there goin'... you know... what... what's goin' - in my head - what's goin' on... and... and I... I got got to thinkin' about it... and I, I get angry at first and then I started thinkin' about it and then when you called back. I'm GLAD you called back. 'Cause then... that way I... I... maybe I could find out more what's wrong with Silvey. 'Cause I firmly believe he belongs in shackles. He should be put in the nut house.

But... You said he's harmless. You see what he's done... you see what he's done to my life. Is that harmless? That is not harm-... No that's not harmless. That's destructive. That screwed my life up. And... it's comin' back. So it's still screwin' it up.

And it just... and it, it just comes back ta'... You... you put... put yourself in my shoes and set there an'... an'... an'... Yeah.

Sure... sure. You... you... you... I mean you set there and this stuff's commin', commin' back. The door's openin' up again. An... an... he yeah, I mean just. I layed in bed with a, with a carbine... with a 60 round CLIP fer 6 MONTHS. I took it to bed and I says... You know I told my... my brother says... NO we didn't know what he was capable. He says "Hey. You've been shootin' at him." I said "WHAT?". I said "I didn't." I got outta' Sunol I left Sunol for 6 months. I had to' hid. My brother hid me out. He said... an' we... you know, just kinda' watched out an he checked on me all the time... an' boy it's just like I say... I, I watched where I went Well... I wasn't used to it. I wasn't used to that, livin' like that because my life's uh never uh like that. And he set there and then... then he put me in a position that I'm, I'm angry. An'

I'm still angry that it comes back up, to the fact that, he put me through hell... fer... prob'ly a year... you know to where finally I go, ok now I talked to the sheriff. I got this information to him. Everythings kinda' cooled off.

en I get up here. I get a phone call... from, from HIM. He... he... and... and then... when he... he calls up... And I says, "Tim, we gotta' do somethin' about this." I says "This crap..." I says "This is not... this is not...". An' I told Tim what happened.

I never could figger' out how... oh wait a minute... let me back up. I DO know how I got involved... the book. It comes back... back up.

That's... that's what really got things goin'... after he read the book. Was seein' that... TA' ME. Now what he told you I have no idea. An', an' I mean... Anyway go ahead I was what? But why? I mean... I... I, I didn't... I didn't know... no, I didn't know him... I... I didn't know him... but why. I don't know how I got fingered. Ha ha ha know him... I... I didn't know him... but why. I don't know how I got fingered. Ha ha ha

Is he wakenin' up... is that what y'er sayin'?

In his eyes... Oh I know... hey I know that... I know he believes it.

Tha' sister of tha', one of tha'... one of tha' victims. Well they want closure... I can... I can understand that.

So this story has really... traveled...

Meaning what?"

INTERVIEW

WITH LEUREN MORET

AND ALFRED LABREMONT WEBRE

COOP RADIO – VANCOUVER B.C. on JULY 23, 2007

CIA: Bastion of Integrity -

William (Wild Bill) Donovan, Coordinator of Information by FDR, recruited a Cornell graduate from Boston named Stanley Lovell. Lovell described his work as follows: "What I have to do is to stimulate the Peck's Bad Boy beneath the surface of every American scientist and say to him, 'Throw all your normal law-abiding concepts out the window. Here's a chance to raise merry hell. Come help me raise it.'"

ALW: This is Vancouver COOP Radio, CFRO 102.7 FM, www.coopradio.org on the internet. This is the Monday Brownbagger. I'm Alfred Webre, and today we have a special guest, Leuren Moret, who's been an expert witness at the Tokyo International Tribunal for war crimes in Afghanistan, as well as a speaker at the Kuala Lumpur War Crimes Conference, and is now an expert witness on depleted uranium issues for a member of the Canadian Parliament. And today we'll be speaking about some recent reseach that Leuren has done in the area of Mind Control and Electronic Harrassment. Welcome Leuren…

LKM: Thank you very much Alfred, it's always a pleasure to be on your program, and to have the privilege of being on COOP Radio.

ALW: One of the concepts that we were exploring was that the development of the technology of mind control actually goes back… well in one significant program to the 70's… to a secret arrangement between the United States and the then Soviet Union. I wonder if you could tell us about that.

LKM: Yes, following World War II the ruling elite or the shadow government in the United States , wanted to pursue a program to develop mind control because they believed that American servicemen who had been prisoners of war in, for instance China and other Asian countries, had returned as sort of mind control victims or zombies. And so John Foster Dulles and Allan Dulles actually set up the CIA in the late 1940's for the purpose of developing mind control programs.

They didn't exactly know what the Asians had done but they wanted to have that ability themselves. And in the 1950's several projects were set up – Project Artichoke and I think Project Bluebird – and these were the precursors of the MK-ULTRA program and they were brought under the umbrella of MK-ULTRA when it was started in... I guess the mid 1950's.

And I didn't know anything about it, I had sort of heard about MK-ULTRA but I really didn't know anything about it, until a Project Artichoke victim approached me and asked me to help him write a book.

And I said "Well why don't you bring all your documentation and your diaries and photos and whatever you have over to my house and I'll look at and if it checks out then of course I'll help you. So I began to learn about MK-ULTRA.

But before that – I'm a nuclear weapons lab whistleblower at the Livermore lab and I'm a geoscientist - so from about the year 2000 I began working 18 hours a day on radiation issues, as a result of visiting the Hiroshima and Nagasaki Museums, and beginning to understand how horrific nuclear weapons are. And I had worked as a staff scientist at the Lawrence Berkeley Lab when it was still conducting nuclear weapons research, although I was studying volcanoes, and then later on in 1989 I was hired at the Lawrence Livermore lab and worked there two years and just quit in utter disgust over the science fraud and contractor [fraud] and all kinds of corruption. And little did I know that actually Livermore had a very important part to play in MK-ULTRA and that's where the software was developed for the global mind control project which George Herbert Walker Bush was the chief architect and CEO beginning when he was in the CIA

He was probably recruited when he was at Yale in Skull and Bones, and he certainly was very early taken into the CIA... and a very important operative, a very nasty one too.

The software for mind control was developed through MK-ULTRA. And there was a monkey colony at U.C. Davis when I was an undergraduate there in the 60's and I always wondered what it was for. I heard stories from roommates and other people who worked there, and they described this very large colony of monkeys that was off the campus and very isolated nobody was allowed over there. But people who worked there and took care of the monkeys told these horrific tales of monkeys running around with the tops of their heads cut off and these wires and electrodes coming out of their brains. It was just really... just... some... some... pathological experiment going on there.

And then the hardware, the antenna, for this global mind control project came out of actually the Soviet Union. And it was discovered in I think the 1960's when... maybe it was the 1950's... when at least three of our US Ambassadors to the Soviet Union died from brain tumors, brain cancer.

And it was the result of the Russians, the Soviets, micro-waving the U.S. Embassy in Moscow and causing not only brain cancer in three Ambassadors or other illnesses. But some of the staff in the Embassy also died of neurological diseases and very strange illnesses. And actually Henry Kissinger, who was in the State Department, stepped in, covered it up, gave the Embassy workers hazard pay, and some of them you know never regained their health. Their health was destroyed.

So on July 4, 1976, the 200th anniversary of the establishment of the United States of America as an independent country, the Woodpecker signal was turned on by the Soviet Union and nobody knew what it was but the ham radio operators around the world picked it up immediately It was a sort of a knocking sound or a pecking sound on their transmissions, on their radio transmissions, and they nicknamed it the "Woodpecker signal" because it sounded like you know Woodpeckers sound when they are pecking on trees. It interfered with airplane and ship traffic [radio communications] on the seas, so the Soviets took out certain bandwidths or frequencies that were interfering with communications that were necessary for airplanes and ships. And it remained in operational mode for quite a long time.

And it turns out that that signal was over the horizon radar transmitted from seven of the largest transmitters in the world located on the eastern side of the Soviet Union and on the Western side. And one of them was powered by Chernobyl - the nuclear power plant at Chernobyl. These consumed huge amounts of electricity and they were transmitting beams of radar – over the horizon radar – which were transmitted all the way to the United States.

And they could cross these beams over each other because the transmitters were a long distance apart in the Soviet Union. And they were conducting experiments with the full cooperation of the U.S. government. In fact they became secret partners in 1978 at a United Nations meeting, which was held… it was a treaty signing conference, where 68 countries signed a treaty agreeing not to use the environment as a weapon, and not to damage the environment with environmental weapons or other kinds of weapons. At that agreement… at that treaty signing agreement the Unites States and the Soviet Union became secret partners in the Woodpecker Project, and also in the development, the co-development of environmental weapons, which we would call exotic weapons today… such as weather modification or weather warfare, tectonic warfare - that's triggering earthquakes and volcanoes erupting, then the mind control is part of that.

ALW: Just to ask you so that for example with regard to the Woodpecker Project, the U.S. then in effect outsourced its program to the Soviet Union and allowed it to attack a specific city…

LKM…and experiment upon American citizens…

ALW: Yeah, and then the U.S. went in and evaluated the results.

LKM: Well actually we sent many scientists and a very very large magnet that weighed many tons, and we also transferred other technology and equipment and money to the Soviet Union. So really in a way you could say they were under contract to us. We also outsourced testing the MK-ULTRA software and experimented on Canadians. Dr. [Ewen] Cameron at… what University was he at?

ALW… McGill University …

LKM: Yes, McGill University. He was actually conducting experiments, MK-ULTRA experiments on Canadian citizens. And they were doing horrific things like erasing their memories and doing just horrible things to their brains and their ability to function as normal human beings. They really destroyed them. This was allowed secretly by the Canadian government.

And the U.S. secretly allowed the Soviets to conduct the hardware experiments with the Woodpecker Project, the transmission of this mind control technology through very very large transmitters in the Soviet Union. And so it most definitely was a joint project between the U.S., Canada, the Soviet Union, and of course… of course… England was deeply involved as well.

ALW: So these are just partners in the permanent war economy.

LKM: These are partners in the permanent war economy and this really involves the Wall Street banking establishment, Skull and Bones – the secret society at Yale where the sons of the Wall Street banking establishment have been members, and rose to very very high and important positions in the secret government, as well as infiltrating the regular government of the United States since even before the 1850's. It involves this partnership between the Wall Street banking establishment, the British Throne, and the London money power, which on the face of it is managed by the Rockefellers…I mean the Rothschilds.

ALW: Going back to the development of the mind control… of the mind control technology. Then how did that relate to Livermore where you were working?

LKM: Well, when I was working there, I was working on the Superfund project to clean up the chemical waste at Livermore from years and years of very sloppy and irresponsible practices of just dumping chemicals all over the property. I had no idea there was radioactive contamination everywhere. I mean I was working as a drilling geologist and sampling 3000 samples a month.

I didn't know they were contaminated with radioactivity. So I quit after two years and just thought it was absolutely the weirdest place I had ever been in my life. There was a very strong social filter there, where mostly people who liked to be controlled survived that social filter, and remained there most of their careers. They sort of thought they were getting free money but what they were getting was free cancer instead. So I had no idea what projects they were doing there. It's completely secret. All the information is compartmentalized. You don't even know what the application is for whatever research you're doing there.

I remember going to the laser building. I had heard about this huge laser project called Shiva. When I entered this very large building they were sort of shooting this laser beam all over this building upstairs and downstairs. they had mirrors sitting on chairs on the top of stairs and at the bottom of stairs You know it was just kids playing with really big toys. And in the lobby of this building was a huge statue of Shiva. It's an Indian god with many arms and legs. To the physicists working on the laser project, it represented the "Dance of the Universe" [Brownian motion]. Later on I discovered in a film about the HAARP Project, now the HAARP Project is around the Arctic Circle and that is where they put the hardware – the Woodpecker signal or the Woodpecker Project together with the MKULTRA software - that is three very large antenna arrays that are over a square mile each and they are located in Alaska, one is in Newfoundland, and one is in Norway. The purpose is to entrain and manipulate the earth's magnetic field with these very very large antennas. Now the way they developed them, was Livermore developed the hardware – the HAARP antenna. The Stanford Research Institute was involved in the MK-ULTRA mind control. And U.C. Davis is where they had the monkey colony where they did experiments and produced research, which was then applied to human beings.

The nexus of the of Livermore-Stanford Research Institute-U.C. Davis activity was actually in Sunol, which is a very very tiny little ranch town with just a few hundreds of people there where the Hearst family, William Randolph Hearst and his family, had a cattle ranch. This is sort of the hub of the wheel that Stanford, Livermore, and U.C. Davis are on. Or they are some distance from this central point. There were CIA people living there, there were Skull and Bones people involved in Sunol, there were Stanford Researchers living there – physicists. It was very convenient to have them all living and socializing in this little town At that time and probably still today, Stanford, Livermore, and UC Berkeley are the two big CIA centers where a lot of operations are going on and of course there's a lot of collaboration.

Dave Silvey, who had been in Project Artichoke... he was kidnapped when he was eight on his birthday, and taken to the safe house.

He showed me a photograph of it. It was just this old farmhouse out in the country. I finally said to him "Well where this safe house is?" He said, "It's in Livermore ..." That's when I knew the Livermore lab had to have been involved in MK-ULTRA and in the HAARP Project, and in the Woodpecker Project.

I finally found an Awards Newsletter where the Livermore lab scientists love to show off and talk about all the prizes and awards they got that year for their research, their "unique" research projects. And in 1993, in that newsletter it said that sixteen Livermore scientists had traveled to NSA headquarters and CIA headquarters, to receive the highest civilian awards that they give. And it was for their Woodpecker Project, which they "couldn't say what it was really about because it was top secret", but it was for "getting information in a way there was no other way to get information". Of course this was about the mind control and mind reading technology we know now after further research.

Dave Silvey described the day he was kidnapped. A priest came up to him as he was walking home and the priest said "Oh your mother wants me to take you to her work today. She can't come and get you, and she sent me to come and fetch you for her. Here just get into the back of the car." And so Dave got in the back of the car and there were no handles on the door at all. He couldn't get out. The priest actually took him to the safe house in Livermore that day.

There were horrible tortures that went on with children in that house. They were raped. Some of them were murdered. They did horrible experiments on them. "Well did they ever put a helmet on your head or electrodes on your head?" He said "Oh yeah, sometimes they would take us upstairs and put us in this big chair like a dentist's chair, and put a helmet on our head, and it had all these wires coming out of it."

Well, when Dave and I and Marion Fulk, who is a Manhattan Project scientist retired from Livermore Lab… when we went out to look at the safe house, there was this huge transformer on a pole right next to the window upstairs, which was the room where these experiments were done. And why in the world would a farmhouse have a huge transformer on a pole next to it, when there no way they would need that kind of electricity, or that much? And the windows are still completely boarded over on all the upstairs windows. And Dave described… one time he escaped. He pushed the… he was locked in the barn, and he and this little girl… she helped him push the boards open away from the barn so that he could crawl out, and he ran away and ended up in this huge antenna field. Well when he told me about the antenna field, I knew that had to also be part of the safe house and what Livermore was actually doing there. The Federal Communications… the FCC actually owned that very large antenna field.

Those antennas are gone now, but after I had gone out to the safe house with Dave Silvey, I took him back to his house and sat him down in front of the computer and I went to the HAARP website in Alaska, and I showed him that facility and he almost had a heart attack. He said "Oh my god... the safe house... we were the prototype for that HAARP facility in Alaska."

ALW: Right... so... so that... actually then, HAARP was developed at Livermore nuclear laboratories.

LKM: That's right and I have actually talked to a scientist who worked at Livermore, and told me he worked on the HAARP Project developing that antenna. And he said "I always wondered why the HAARP Project was so well funded every year... year after year." He was there like in the 70's. And he said "There was no obvious benefit to the public... from this project."

ALW: Right... and so that was the hardware of this vast mind control weapon.

LKM: That's right.

ALW: The software... where was that developed, again?

LKM: That was the MK-ULTRA Projects that involved almost every person in the American Psychiatry Association [correction: American Psychological Association (APA)] and also many many electrical engineers. There's a very big organization for electrical engineers [Institute of Electrical and Electronics Engineers (IEEE)] and they actually published a book of research papers that pertained to the MK-ULTRA/HAARP Project. So, Academia has been a key player in the development of the MK-ULTRA software, and the HAARP antenna, or the electronic hardware.

It's very interesting that in the 1850's, Dwight and Gilman, who were two "Bonesmen" from Skull and Bones at Yale, came out to California, and Dwight [correction: Daniel Gilman] was appointed as the first President of the University of California. And Dwight and Gilman were very busy at UC Berkeley. And they actually set up the land grant college system in the United States, which is where the bureaucrats and the flunkies for the ruling elite and the shadow government are trained. The sons of the wealthy ruling elite and the Wall Street banking establishment go to Yale and to Harvard (but the Harvard men serve the Yale men), and to Princeton and other Ivy League colleges. So there is even, and especially through Academia... Academic institutions... are where the real framework of this apparatus has been set up.

ALW: Right... now, now for example what... what would be the application of the HAARP Project to the population of Canada? How is HAARP applied here in Canada?

LKM: Well... Canada and the United States are really economic colonies of Britain. The British Empire is certainly not dead. It's very much alive. And so I think that you and I observed on our recent speaking tour of SE Asia that the U.S. military presence is just everywhere, or in almost every country we went to.

But I think we agreed at the end of our trip that the U.S. military is just the military bully or proxy for the Zionist Anglo-American Economic Empire. So whatever is developed in the U.S. and in Canada is really developed to benefit the British throne and the London money power or banking establishment. They're the ones who are really running the world.

And so, what they desired to do, was to develop these technologies to be able to dominate and subdue their own citizens, with the global population as well, in order to carry out their goals, and implement their goals, which was... its basic communism. It's a one-class system all over the planet with one central government running everything. Depopulation is a very very key part of this, because they want to depopulate by 1/3 to 2/3 of the world population – in other words 2-4 billion people. And as crazy and outrageous as that statement sounds, it's actually in the National Security Council memos from their meetings. It became National Security policy in a paper called "GLOBAL 2000" which Kissinger, Zbiegnew Brzezinski, General Alexander Haig, and Ed Muskie wrote for President Carter in 1979. In the National Security Council meetings, in the minutes or the memos from those meetings leading up to the creation of this document or this policy paper, Kissinger stated that... depopulation in third world countries in order to control valuable mineral resources was of a greater priority even than the nuclear weapons program to U.S. National Security.

ALW: Right... so bring this back around to Canada in terms of the HAARP hardware, and the MKULTRA software, which is...

HAARP is a delivery system for mind control software. And there are other applications of HAARP as well. How would you imagine that this weapon is now being used in Canada and against Canada?

LKM: Some of the key times that it would be used... what I've observed in the United States, is there is very heavy use of it during elections. It's turned on at night and transmitted through police towers, and cell phone towers, but also they can transmit it from HAARP around the Arctic circle. The chemtrails that people have observed are actually being used as electromagnetic frequency mirrors, and the transmissions from HAARP are bounced off of these chemtrail mirrors down onto populations that they wish to target. The police antennas are hooked up intimately with satellites, with HAARP, and they all are integrated and overlapping and operate wherever they want to target someone. And they can use them on individuals or they can target large populations.

For instance, they were used in Afghanistan and in Iraq during those wars. When they targeted Iraqi soldiers they could make them feel like their heads were exploding and they would just run off the battlefields and give up.

The Soviets transmitted this mind control from Kazakhstan, and they used it on their own soldiers in Afghanistan towards the end of the Soviet occupation of Afghanistan when the Russian soldiers were so demoralized and depressed. They actually transmitted mood control to lift their spirits and to empower them, and to put them in a more positive psychological state.

Now, the way they are using them on Canadians and Americans is they can target individuals who are protestors, whistleblowers, change agents, people like you and me, and a lot of people that we know. They also have targeted especially single women because they're more vulnerable. I know they practiced on prisoners. Now there are actual formal contracts between universities, colleges, and private institutions under new legislation that has been passed since 1993 in the United States including the Patriot Act. And there is a standing contract between these educational institutions and Homeland Security, the military, and law enforcement.

This software and hardware and technologies, combined with sociological behavior like gang stalking, are being tested under contract in universities, colleges and private institutions. I believe the very worst institution carrying out this kind of research is the University of California.

They have fourteen campuses in California. And I have observed at U.C. Davis, and U.C.L.A., and at U.C. Berkeley, on the U.C. campuses I have been on, and U.C. Santa Cruz, that the students are actively participating with faculty members. They are experimenting on un-... other... unwitting or naive faculty members and other students. They're tracking them, targeting them, gang stalking them. It's really disgusting... And what's very funny is that this activity was being observed at one college campus and the police antenna suddenly failed, from a power failure. All of a sudden the students and the faculty member were very confused. They just stopped... they had been gang stalking a target, and they sort of got... they sort of scurried off like cockroaches.

You know, they didn't know what to do, and they also didn't know what they had been doing. So, these patterns of behavior are obviously being transmitted from the police antennas.

ALW: Now... when you say gang stalking, for the members of our COOP Radio audience who may not be familiar with that, could you describe that?

LKM: Well I observed gang stalking on the U.C. Davis campus, and

I was also targeted at U.C. Davis and at U.C. Berkeley, but it was very very bad there. Chancellor Vanderhoef, who has raised a lot of money for the campus and is a particularly disgusting individual, even his own grown adult son was involved in the gang stalking. They have hundreds of people who are involved in it and these are at all levels of the university – from the top, the Chancellor's family, all the way down to the mechanics, or the gardeners, or the janitors... whatever... it's happening.

It's a pathological institution when this kind of behavior sets in and is condoned and encouraged. And it's used for social and political control. It came out of the Catholic Church. The Masons use it.

The Ku Klux Klan got this gang stalking behavior and technology from the Masons, and it's been used for millennia to control people. It's just more high-tech now with the HAARP and MK-ULTRA new technology that's been developed, but it's the same old stuff...

Bottom of Form

In conclusion an old Talmudic saying "We do not see things as they are, we see them as we are".

The beast who was the evil genius of Zodiac died in Las Vegas in spring of 1977. Dr. William J. Bryan was the master mind behind the random serial killer hoax.

Cherri Jo Bates: In October 1966 Tom had grown a beard and was driving a 1952 tan/gray Studebaker Commander full dress with a window-mounted water cooler and gray exterior sun visor. Tom opened the trunk and I could see antiques such as candleholders and jewelry inside. Tom spoke about being accused of arson for small fires in Sunol. He stated, "I got to kill some motherfucker over that." Trying to change the subject, as I had ratted on him to the Sheriff's Department months before, I asked if he was home for good. He stated "That I am going to college down in Southern California and might have a job, down there, with Bob's (Hemphill's) relative in the maintenance department at Riverside City College. Gene, Bob's friend, is looking into some work at Lockheed for me too."

Riverside PD recreated the scene at the library the night of the murder in 1966. "We had them wear the same clothes, sit in the same seats, park in the same places. Captain Cross's own car doubled for the Bate's auto. We asked them what time they arrived, what people they saw outside, where they parked and what vehicles they noticed. We asked them to tell us if they recalled seeing anyone who was here the night of the killing and didn't come in to be questioned. We tape recorded all interviews. The Captain himself took fingerprints and a lock of hair from each man... The FBI got the prints and we sent the hair samples to CI&I."

"We got two missing, a woman and a heavyset young man about five feet eleven inches tall, with a beard. We were out to find any young man with scratches on his face. We never found either of them or the 47-52 tan-gray Studebaker with oxidized paint that was seen that night".

Below is a picture of the '52 Studebaker now with gray spray can oxidize paint. The accessories and motor are missing. Tom Pain was driving this car in the summer and fall of 1966, now abandoned next to Gene Cesar's oxidized lime green '47 Studebaker in Sunol...

Also in 1966, friend or relative of Bob's confronted me in the driveway of 187 Kilkare. He was WMA, in his twenty, 5'10', and 175 lbs. with light brown hair. He was angry and wanted to fight...

"So you're the son of a bitch, I know your family well. Bob is sick in the head, what's wrong with you? You don't see that Bob is nuts and he is driving his mother nuts. He steals money from her to buy your damn dope. We suspect that he may have killed a girl. If you don't stay away from him, I'll call the police and have you arrested. If I have to turn Bob in, you and that long hair punk are going to jail". I felt terrible we knew the LSD was going to be trouble with this nut, to think that it got a girl killed. It caused me to write this stuff down. Bob was relentless, he is scary.

Darlene Ferrin: Darlene had knowledge of CIA Artichoke team involvement in the conspiracy to induce a subject, under influence of Artichoke, to perform an involuntary act of attempted assassination against Senator Robert F. Kennedy. The act was one of distraction, while a cold blooded assassin actually killed the Senator. The fact that Ferrin was a witness and participant became the motive to dispose of her.

"Ferrin is the key to solving the Zodiac murders. But she is also the key to proving that the Zodiac was a hoax he was not a random killer, he killed for a purpose. Darlene had indicated that a big story would break in the newspapers around July 5, 1969. Ferrin also apparently knew her assailant according to several witnesses, including Michael Mageau, who was shot along side of Ferrin on July 4, 1969. When asked if he could give a description of the man, Mike said he appeared to be short, possibly 5'8, about 26 to 30 in real age, real heavy set with a beefy build, possibly 195-200 lbs. or maybe even larger. He had short curly hair, light brown, almost blonde, and was wearing a short-sleeved shirt, blue in color. There was nothing unusual about his face, other than it appeared to be large. He did not have a mustache, nor was he wearing glasses."

A good description of Gene Cesar; a Cuban Kennedy hater and armed security guard at the Ambassador Hotel the night of the assassination. If Gene Cesar is indeed Robert Kennedy's assassin no one had a better motive to silence Darlene. Bob Hemphill harassed Darlene just before the shooting but then has an air tight alibi at the exact time of the attack. ." Gene Cesar is living in the Philippines.

July 31, 1969 the San Francisco Chronicle, the San Francisco Examiner and the Vallejo Times received letters from her killer. Zodiac was introduced in a three-page letter in the part that was sent to the Vallejo Times Herald. August 1, 1969 the San Francisco Chronicle received a cryptogram from

Zodiac. In the last line is code name 'Bob Hemphill,' but on the 4th line is his real name as it appears on the Zodiac suspect list. San Francisco Police Inspector Dave Toschi received a Zodiac cryptogram on November 8, 1969 that the NSA, CIA and FBI code breakers and computers couldn't solve.

In the un-decoded 340-symbol Zodiac cipher the first number is the number of rows, and the second number in the coordinate is the number of rows to the right, (4, 15) is 4 rows down and 15 rows to the right - 'RK.' 'K' is at the coordinate (4, 16). The date RFK was assassinated '6/5' is coordinate (6, 5) 'F' the missing middle initial for 'RK.'[Bookworm, see zodiackiller.com - part of strand, internet entry 2003 approx] On the 10th row of the decoded version appears 'H LSD UL.' positioned at the center. In most CIA medical documentation H is the abbreviation for hypnosis, together with LSD UL it could possibly be referring to extremely sensitive and at the time Top-Secret, MK-ULTRA behavioral modification technique. Combine un-decoded with decoded elements from center line of cryptogram the message is clear.

RFK ASSASINATED UTILIZING LETHAL
HYPNOSIS LSD - [ARTICHOKE].

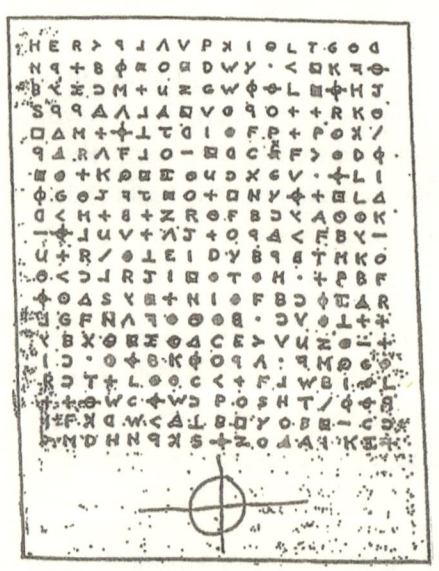

DECODED VERSION
HERB CAIN
I GIVE THEM HELL TOO.
BLAST THESE LIES. SLUETH
SHOELD [SHOULD] SEE A NAME
BELOW KILLERS FILM. APILLS
GAME. ARDON ME ACCEPT TO
BLAST NE [ME]. BULLSHIT.
THESE FOOLS SHALL MEET
KILLER. PLEAS ASK LUNBLAD.

SOEL [SOUL] AT H LSD UL
CLEAR LAKE. SO STARE I
EAT A PILL, ASSHOLE. I
PLANT MR A. H. PHONE LAKE B.

Darlene lived in a boarding house-type facility. According to Darlene's family, that boarding house or resident hotel was on Eddy Street. Also briefly living there was Paul Stine, a yellow Cab driver who was a claimed Zodiac victim. The suspect was associated with the residential hotel in San Francisco on Eddy Street. Darlene's first husband was resident of the residential hotel. It was through this facility, that Darlene met Michael Mageau, the man who was also shot on the night of July 4, 1969.

Paul Stine: October 11, 1969: At 3898 Washington Street in San Francisco three teenagers watched from the second floor windows approximately 50 feet away as the assailant struggled with the cab driver after shooting him in the head. Two patrolmen arrived and questioned a man some blocks away from the scene but did not detain him. The composite poster generated later by eyewitness accounts was incredibly accurate on both men. Most believe it to be an amended composite of one man 'Zodiac' The witness's and patrolman did an excellent job on their descriptions, Tom Pain on the left side and Bob Hemphill on the right.

In the fall of 1970 Tom Pain bragged that he left the city covered in the cabdriver's blood. "Bob never got close enough to the scene to be noticed and had no blood on his clothing when a few minutes later two patrolman drove up." The perpetrators Bob Hemphill and Tom Pain are both still living in Northern California.

Amnesty for the handles and clemency for criminal acts conducted by government induced Manchurian Candidates maybe the only way to identify unknown victims to begin reconciling the evil. The MK-ULTRA legacy is like a mine disaster with so many souls lost inside, it's not hard to subscribe to theory that we are all just puppets of fate, but if we do, indeed we are.

Dave Silvey

www.ingramcontent.com/pod-product-compliance
Lightning Source LLC
Chambersburg PA
CBHW020433290526
45785CB00002B/826